ccess with

Soft Fruits

CHRISTINE RECHT

Series Editor:
LESLEY YOUNG

MEREHURST

Foreword

Raspberries, strawberries, red and blackcurrants and all the other delicious berry fruits can only really be enjoyed if they are harvested without a coating of chemical spray or other plant protection substances.
For this reason you should always grow soft fruits organically, whether you have grown them in the garden or in a large container on your patio or balcony. The most important points about growing soft fruits organically are explained here by Christine Recht in an easy-to-follow way, even for the beginner. The most important thing of all is to place the right plant in the right position. The choice of variety is also important as is the type of soil available and the climate. With the help of this guide, choosing the right varieties is made easy thanks to excellent photographs and detailed instructions on the care of many varieties of soft fruit that will grow well in a garden or on a patio or balcony. Clear instructions and step-by-step illustrations of plant care will help the reader to become a successful soft fruit gardener. This guide emphasises the use of biological plant protection and includes the use of preventive measures employing herbal brews and infusions as well as the encouragement of useful insects in the garden. These environmentally safe, tried and tested methods ensure that the use of toxic sprays will be quite unnecessary, that the fruit will taste better and the harvest be more abundant.

Contents

Cultivated cranberries.

White grapes.

Strawberries – straw laid underneath will prevent them from getting dirty.

The author
Christine Recht is co-editor of several specialist gardening magazines and the author of a number of successful books on topics such as herbs in cooking, large container plants, houseplants and growing fruit trees.

Cover photographs
Front cover: *Redcurrant "Heinemanns Rote Spätlese".*
Inside front cover: *Raspberry "Glen Glora".*
Inside back cover: *Soft fruit in pots and large containers.*
Back cover: *Strawberry barrel.*

Important: Please read the Author's Note on page 63.

Sweet berries from your own garden

Delicious strawberries, redcurrants, raspberries and gooseberries in the summer, grapes and elderberries in the autumn and kiwi fruit during the winter – there is always room in a garden for soft fruit that is rich in vitamins. Many species can even be grown on a patio or balcony.

Berries are one of our oldest foodstuffs. Archaeological finds from the Stone Age prove that people collected berries thousands of years ago as an important part of their diet. Basically, nothing much has changed to this day. Berries still give variety in our diet and provide essential vitamins, minerals and trace elements. They can be eaten raw and fresh or cooked, processed and preserved in many different ways.

What are berries?
Generally speaking, we refer to all small, soft, sweet fruits as berries even if a botanist would classify them differently by distinguishing them as:

- genuine berries which grow as single fruits (blueberries, gooseberries); in bunches (red/blackcurrants, grapes); or in umbels (elderberry)
- fruits with stones which grow singly (sloe) or form aggregates of many tiny fleshy drupes, each containing a tiny stone or pip (raspberries, blackberries)
- plants which bear many tiny, nut-like seeds (achenes embedded in a fleshy receptacle), such as strawberries.

NB: In the countryside many wild bushes also bear berries. These are often inedible by humans and provide food only for birds. Berries that are used for consumption by people are referred to as "soft fruits".

Berry plants: Berries grow on bushes, trees, leafy plants and creepers. As well as the older berry plants which have been cultivated by people for centuries, such as raspberries, red/blackcurrants and strawberries, an increasing number of exotic berries now invade our gardens. Probably the best known is the kiwi fruit, but sugar cherries, passion fruit and other exotic fruits are also gaining ground. In addition, there are the crosses between well-known berry varieties, like the jostaberry (a cross between a blackcurrant and a gooseberry) and the tayberry whose parents are the blackberry and the raspberry. Cultivated blueberries and cranberries are now quite different from their wild ancestors of the forests. Even garden strawberries are now often crosses between American varieties.

Shapes of fruit: *1 achenes embedded in a fleshy receptacle (strawberry); 2 fleshy drupes, each with a pip (raspberry); 3 genuine berry (blueberry).*

NB: The hazelnut, as its name indicates, is a nut not a berry. Nevertheless, we shall introduce it in this text as it has similar requirements to berries with respect to soil and care, is just as popular and there should be room for it in any garden.

Redcurrant standard
Standards are easy to integrate within an ornamental garden. Nasturtiums make a good underplanting.

How berries grow

Not only can berries look very different from each other, they also grow on plants which come in a wide range of shapes and have differing requirements.
It is mainly the low-growing, leafy plants, like strawberries, blueberries and cranberries, that are cultivated **in beds**. Of course, this does not mean that you have to grow these plants in straight rows like cabbages or lettuces. For example, blueberries and cranberries can be inegrated as part of an ornamental garden or you can plant certain varieties of strawberries on a bank or in a border.
Bushes like red/blackcurrants, gooseberries and jostaberries, and even raspberries grown on individual canes, are referred to as bush-grown soft fruits even if they do not have the typical bush-like shape of growth.
Other bush-grown soft fruits with long rambling shoots can be grown on espaliers, for example blackberries, grapes and kiwi fruit. ***Espaliers*** can be trained against a house wall or the wall of a shed or garage. They can even be free-standing as is often seen in vineyards. Blackberries and raspberries can also be grown like this, although kiwi fruit grown as a free-standing espalier would lack sufficient support for the large heavy fruit. A stable pergola is more suitable for them.
Of all the berries that are grown in Europe, elderberries are the main crop harvested from trees. Other, more recently rediscovered berries, like mulberries and the edible rowan (*Sorbus domestica*), also grow as trees, as do *Aronia melanocarpa* and figs.

Wild berries in your garden

Basically, all berries are descended from wild plants and some of them can still be gathered in the wild, such as blueberries, blackberries, woodland strawberries, cranberries and elderberries. These wild berries have an incomparable flavour which may tempt one to bring plants from the wild into one's garden. Try to resist such an impulse, as such plants will not enrich your garden and their removal from their natural habitats will only leave the environment poorer. Our countryside is already damaged enough without gardeners plundering it. Also, wild berries will only develop their true flavour where the type of soil, mini-climate and the entire biotope combine to provide the best possible conditions. Such plants would probably wither and die in your garden. The only plants that might be marginally successful are wild strawberries, but it is much preferable to purchase cultivated woodland strawberries.

The amount of fruit that can be harvested annually

Species	Amount of fruit	Plant/bush
blackberries	1-2 kg (2-5 lb)	per plant
blackcurrants	3-5 kg (7-11 lb)	per bush
blueberries	2-3 kg (5-7 lb)	per plant
cranberries	100-200 g (3 -7½ oz)	per plant
elderberry	10-30 kg (22-66 lb)	per tree
gooseberries	5-8 kg (11-18 lb)	per bush
hazelnuts	2-5 kg (5-11 lb)	per bush
jostaberries	5-8 kg (11-18 lb)	per bush
kiwi fruit	10-30 kg (22-66 lb)	per plant
raspberries	500 g-1 kg (18 oz-2 lb)	per cane
red/whitecurrants	2-8 kg (5-18 lb)	per bush
strawberries	500-800 g (18-28 oz)	per plant

Know your plants!

This book is about growing edible soft fruits. If you also have ornamental shrubs and bushes in your garden which bear toxic berries, you will have to be very careful indeed. Toxic berries tend to look just as appetizing as edible ones, and the danger to children is very great if they become confused about which is which! If you have small children, you should avoid planting ornamental shrubs that produce berries as most pretty berries are just too tempting!
Among the most common ornamental shrubs with attractive berries are : spindleberry (*Euonymus europaea*), mezereon (*Daphne mezereum*), yew (*Taxus*), varieties of honeysuckle (*Lonicera*), privet (*Ligustrum*), snowball bush (*Viburnum opulus*), holly (*Ilex*) and cotoneaster. Always consider the possible risks before purchasing these plants.

Ten good reasons for growing soft fruit

Many varieties of berry can be purchased in supermarkets and from fruit stalls but there are still good reasons for growing soft fruits in your own garden or even on a patio or balcony.

A group of plants that like acid soil: cranberries, heathers and pine.

1 Home-grown berries are cheaper. Most varieties of soft fruit will yield crops for many years. The purchase price of the plant will have been recouped by the second year of harvesting.
2 Some soft fruit varieties are seldom seen for sale, for example alpine strawberries, elderberries and certain raspberries.
3 Soft fruits taste best when freshly picked as lengthy transportation and storage are avoided. As they have very juicy, soft flesh, they inevitably suffer some damage through storage or unprofessional transportation.
4 Your own home-grown berries can be eaten fresh or processed immediately. When you buy berries, they have often been harvested when still only half-ripe (for transportation purposes) or have been sitting on the shelf for several days.
5 Your home-grown soft fruit will be much tastier. This is partly because it will not be harvested until it is completely ripe and also because it will not have been forced with artificial fertilizer.
6 You can be sure that soft fruit from your garden has not been treated with chemical agents. Such agents are necessary for the commercial market but at home you can use natural agents.
7 If you grow your own soft fruit, you can choose early, medium and late varieties.
8 Soft fruits from your own garden can be harvested in quantities to suit your needs.
9 Your own harvest has not been handled by several people, as is the case with bought fruit.
10 Many soft fruit plants are real ornaments in your garden, either because they have attractive flowers or because of their colourful autumn foliage.

A place in the sun

Most kinds of soft fruit will give you much pleasure for many years but there are a few points to consider carefully before you buy anything. How will you integrate the plant into your garden? What position will it require? And, of course, which type of fruit and how many plants can you accommodate?

With few exceptions, soft fruit bushes will yield fruit for many years, even decades. The most important factor is the right position. Soft fruit plants like to soak up as much sunlight as possible, the soil should meet their requirements and, as far as possible, they need to be provided with the right conditions for their characteristic way of growing. If you provide your soft fruit plants with ideal conditions from the start, you can avoid the use of chemical plant protection agents. Choosing the right position can be seen as your first preventive measure against attack by fungi or pests.

Warm, sunny conditions

Nearly all soft fruit species grow in the kind of warm climate one would find in the wine growing areas of Europe. The only exceptions to this are kiwi fruit and blackberries which require lots of warmth and long summers for ripening. Cranberries, on the other hand, prefer a fresher climate. However, all berries like a warm, sunny position as this will help them to develop their typical flavour and plenty of sugar.

The mini-climate of a particular spot is not always suitable for soft fruits. Observe your garden and you will find that the mini-climates are not the same throughout the garden. There will be draughty spots and some that are sheltered from the wind and become particularly warm. Even the amount of sunlight can vary considerably.

Warmth and sunlight are particularly important. Apart from raspberries, which will flourish even in semi-shade, and gooseberries, which like a little shade during the hotter part of the day, you should always plant soft fruit in the warmest, sunniest spots in the garden. If you decide to grow your strawberries in the vegetable garden, you will have to make sure that tall plants do not create too much shade. Soft fruits that can be grown as espaliers on house walls should always be planted in a south- or west-facing position and only on a south-facing wall in more exposed areas. Free-standing espaliers can be used for blackberries, raspberries and redcurrants. These espaliers should, if possible, be placed in a north-south direction so that the berries benefit from sunlight all day long.

As a rule, ***wind*** will not harm soft fruits but if there is a constant draught it will also be cool and that will delay the ripening process. In addition, constant wind will tend to dry out the soil, which will considerably and detrimentally affect the development of strawberries. In very windy positions, pollination will be affected as bees and other insects will tend not to visit these plants so frequently.

All soft fruit plants require ***moisture***. If there are periods of sustained drought, the berries will remain small or may even dry up. In particular, soft fruits that grow along house walls often do not receive sufficient water so water will have to be supplied regularly.

The need for humus-rich soil

The best fruit yields come from plants grown on loose, permeable soil containing plenty of nutrients. In dense, compacted soil, the roots will not be able to form properly or spread out. In sandy soils, nutrients tend to be used up very quickly. The soil should be very well prepared before planting soft fruit. Heavy soils should be loosened up, preferably a year before planting, by growing leguminous plants (like lupins, sweet peas, beans and peas) on the site. These plants are able to loosen up the soil through the growth of their roots which grow up to 2 m (80 in) long. Very dense soils should be planted with leguminous plants or potatoes for two years before planting soft fruits, in order to loosen the soil.

Very sandy soils should be improved by the addition of ripe compost, well-rotted manure and grit.

My tip: Before planting soft fruits, you should have your soil analysed by sending off a sample to a laboratory which provides this facility (ask for the address of such a service at your local garden centre) or by using a soil analysis kit yourself. This is the only way to find out the proportions of nitrogen, phosphorus, potassium and magnesium that exist in your soil. A good soil laboratory report will also tell you how you can balance any deficiencies or excess in the soil. Your soft fruit will be given an excellent start if you prepare the soil properly. It will then thrive, produce good fruit and, above all, it will be less susceptible to pests and diseases. It is also a good idea to have another soil analysis done if you intend to plant young fruit bushes after removing older bushes or plants.

Soft fruit in the garden

Soft fruit bushes and plants can be planted anywhere in the garden – they will flourish in a vegetable garden or an ornamental garden. Some will even manage in a large container on a patio or balcony.

A vegetable garden

This is the usual place for soft fruit. Strawberries can be grown in rows in beds – spaces between the strawberry plants can be utilized for onions, garlic, radishes and lettuces. Cultivated blueberries can also be grown in beds but cranberries will not flourish in very nutrient-rich soils. Red/white/blackcurrants, jostaberries and gooseberries can be planted along a garden boundary or as a hedge in an ornamental garden but may also be planted individually. A hedge espalier can also be used as a boundary. This is the usual method of growing raspberry canes which can be tied to a fence. Alpine strawberries can be planted as a border of a bed as they do not produce runners. An elderberry bush or tree may be used to provide shade for the composting corner of the garden.

A rustic garden

Soft fruits are a common sight in a traditional rustic garden. They are particularly attractive when grown as standards. They may be used as the centrepiece of a roundel or to create an avenue down the central path. Standards do not take up as much space as bushes but nor do they yield quite as much fruit. Harvesting and care are simple as there is no need to bend down. A garden gate can have an arch with a grapevine growing on it. Blackberries can be trained along a fence but they have to be cut back rigorously otherwise they will form an impenetrable thicket.

An ornamental garden

Soft fruits can be integrated successfully in an ornamental garden, particularly if they have attractive flowers or foliage. Among such plants is the kiwi fruit which can be trained along a house wall or over a pergola. Blueberries planted in groups can be most attractive, while cranberries will feel quite at home in a rockery.
Red/white/blackcurrants, gooseberries and jostaberries can look good in an ornamental garden and standards are always most decorative. Blackberry varieties without thorns are ideal for training over a pergola or an arch; hazel bushes are more suitable for creating a hedge. Last but not least, a summerhouse with a grapevine trained over it can look quite magnificent.

Space requirements of soft fruit plants

The area indicated (length by width) is what a mature plant will require.

Soft fruit type	Area required per plant
blackberry	4 x 1 m (160 in)
blueberry	1.5 x 1.5 m (60 x 60 in)
cranberry	20 x 25 cm (8 x 10 in)
elderberry	5 x 5 m (200 x 200 in)
gooseberry	1.5 x 1.5 m (60 x 60 in) (standard less)
grapevine	3 x 1 m (120 x 40 in)
hazelnut	5 x 5 m (200 x 200 in)
jostaberry	1.5 x 1.5 m (60 x 60 in)
kiwi fruit	3 x 2 m to 4 x 2 m (120 x 80 in to 160 x 80 in)
raspberry	50 x 100 cm (20 x 40 in)
red/black/whitecurrant	black: 2 x 2 m (80 x 80 in) red and white: 1.5 x 1.5 m (60 x 60 in) – 1.8 x 1.8 m (72 x 72 in)(standard less)
strawberry	30 x 30 cm (12 x 12 in) (alpine 25 x 25 cm/10 x 10 in)

Attractive presentation

Soft fruit plants not only provide delicious fruit – if they are planted in the right positions they can be extremely decorative. Various ways of displaying plants are shown here.

NB: Wooden stakes will rot in moist soil in a few years' time. If the stakes are meant to support plants for many years, specially treated wood is recommended. The parts of the wood that are above ground can also be protected against dampness with non-toxic preparations.

An espalier on a house wall

Kiwi plants, grapevines and blackberries can be trained on an espalier along a house wall. As long as the fruits of the kiwi plant or grapevine are not heavy, the plants will support themselves. Blackberries should be tied to the wall. If you want to build a grid, use dowels to fix strong wooden battens to the wall, spacing them at approximately 1.5 m (5 ft) intervals on 3 cm (1¼ in) thick spacer blocks. Stretch further battens or plastic-clad wire horizontally from one batten to the other, the first one being 60 cm (2 ft) from the ground, with the other wires spaced at 50 cm (20 in) intervals.

A raspberry espalier

Vertically growing raspberry canes will definitely require a supporting grid, otherwise they will fall over or break off. Drive strong wooden stakes, about 2 m (80 in) long, into the soil at intervals of about 2-4 m (80-160 in) (or use iron stakes or concrete posts). At intervals of about 60 cm (24 in), stretch across two or three horizontal wires to which the raspberry canes can be tied. Instead of wire you can also use special raspberry tapes (obtainable in the gardening trade). The canes can be fixed to these using plastic ties, tied firmly but not too tightly.

A V-shaped espalier

A V-shaped espalier is suitable for raspberries, blackberries, red/white/blackcurrants and gooseberries. The advantage is that the canes do not grow too close together and will receive sunlight from all sides. The young shoots of raspberries tend to grow vertically on the inside.

1 Kiwi fruit and grapevines find it easy to cling to an espalier on a house wall but blackberries have to be tied on.

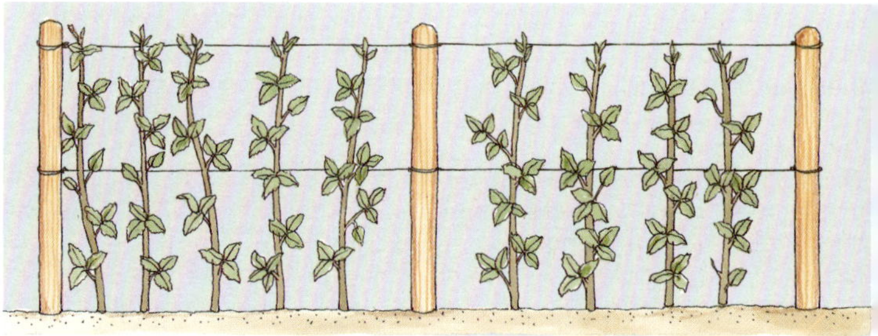

2 Raspberries require a support to prevent them from falling over. The canes are tied singly to the horizontal wires.

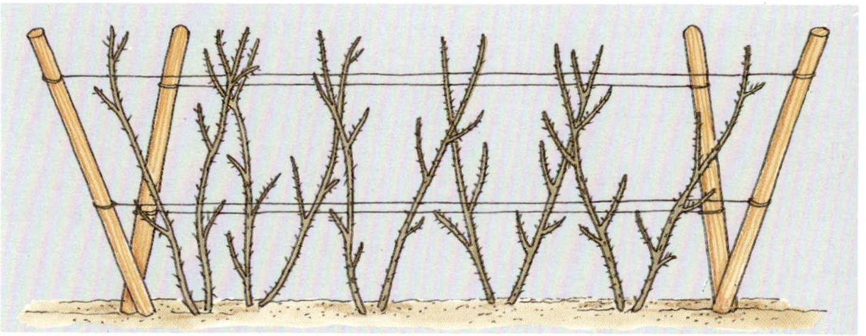

3 A V-shaped espalier is suitable for many types of soft fruit. The canes or shoots can be tied loosely to it and will receive plenty of light.

You can build a V-shaped espalier by hammering two sets of strong stakes made of wood or metal into the ground about 4 m (160 in) apart and anchoring them well. The two stakes that form the V should be connected by means of strong wire at each end so that they are unable to tip over under the weight of the plants. Draw other wires longways at approximately 60 cm (24 in) intervals between the stakes and tie the shoots or canes to these wires.

Soft fruit standards
(illustration 4)
Red/white/blackcurrants, gooseberries and jostaberries can be purchased as standards. Grown in this shape, they will require less space and are also easier to care for and to pick fruit from as you will not need to bend down. Two disadvantages are that the harvest is smaller and that the small trees rarely live for longer than nine or ten years.

Two points to note

- Standards will always require a support stake but better still are three stakes set in a triangle formation which reaches right up to the crown of the tree.
- If three stakes are used, they should be joined by means of short battens. This will also help to support the branches under the full weight of fruit and prevent them from breaking off.

A strawberry barrel
(illustration 5)
Strawberries can be grown even without a garden. A good solution for a patio or balcony is a strawberry barrel.
Bore drainage holes in the bottom of a barrel made of plastic or wood. Place a 15 cm (6 in) thick layer of gravel in the bottom.

4 A standard with a support reaching up to the crown.

5 Strawberries can be grown in a barrel on a patio or balcony.

Cut out holes with a diameter of about 10 cm (4 in) in the sides of the barrel at intervals of about 20 cm (8 in).
Stand a roll of fine-mesh wire or one made of cardboard in the centre of the barrel to facilitate watering and then fill this roll with gravel.
Gradually add garden soil or strawberry compost to the barrel and, as you go, place the strawberry plants in the "pockets". The soil will not dry out so quickly with this method of planting and you will be able to keep it sufficiently moist by adding water from above. If this is done only by filling the central gravel tube with water, the moisture will be evenly distributed throughout the barrel and to all the plants.
You can also purchase ready-to-use strawberry barrels with side pockets (see p. 23). In these the plants can easily be watered from the outside. Strawberry plants with large fruits will not grow well in the limited amount of soil in such pockets, however, so we only recommend growing varieties with small fruits in this type of arrangement.
NB: The plant roots will not be able to spread out as well in a barrel as they would in a garden. This means that the harvest will not be as abundant in the second year. The barrel should be emptied after the second year and the strawberry plants replaced with new young plants after mixing the soil thoroughly with fresh compost.

A strawberry hanging container
Hanging strawberry plants, on whose shoots small plants and berries develop, have been for sale in the gardening trade for some time now. They flourish best in a hanging container that is sufficiently large (volume of at least 5 litres/1 gal).

Berries in a container
Various types of soft fruit plants can also be grown in a sufficiently large pot or container on a patio or balcony. The most suitable plants for this method are

standard red/white/blackcurrant or gooseberry bushes. Other plants suitable for a large container are blueberries.

Buying soft fruit plants

In principle, you should not buy any soft fruit plants until you have prepared a place for them. The roots of all soft fruit plants should never be allowed to dry out. If the plants arrive before you are ready for them, you should stand the roots in water, or temporarily heel in strawberry plants.

Questions to ask

- Is this variety resistant to disease?
- How big will the plant grow?
- Is this variety an early, medium-early or late one? (If you mix the plants, you will have an adequate crop over a longer timespan.)
- Is the variety suitable for the climate where I live?
- In the case of strawberries, are the plants from virus-free plant stock or plants propagated using the meristem system? Only buy plants guaranteed free of disease.

What to watch for

- Has the plant got healthy shoots; that is, light-coloured, undamaged stems and fresh shoot tips?
- Is the rootstock moist right through? If watering has not been done properly, do not buy.
- In the case of strawberries, is the heart of the plant healthy-looking? Are the roots light-coloured and undamaged; the leaves free of spots?
- If you are given cuttings by a friend, have a good look at the parent plant – raspberry cane disease, for example, is transmitted through a larva which lives in the rootstock. Diseases of strawberry plants can also be passed on.

Thornless blackberries can be grown on espaliers and pergolas.

Planting properly is half the battle

If you grow soft fruit plants in your garden, you can look forward to a rich harvest of fruit for many years to come. The ultimate foundation for success, however, is laid down during the first few days – when planting. Only if you take into account correct spacing, planting depth and the right kind of soil, will you enjoy abundant fruit crops for a long time to come.

Many young soft fruit plants are offered for sale in containers and could be planted any time from spring to late summer. However, it is as well to aim for one of the ideal planting times, when young plants tend to root particularly well or when they will be better protected from late frosts.

The right times to plant

Early autumn: Until the end of the first month of autumn, plant red/white/blackcurrants, raspberries, jostaberries, blueberries, cranberries, hazelnuts and elderberry trees. This is the time when the young plants will be able to form proper roots which they will use in early spring for obtaining nutrients and water from the soil.

Early spring, and not before the middle of the first month of spring in areas with severe winters, you can plant the following soft fruits: red/white/blackcurrants, gooseberries and jostaberries. They will not form shoots quite as quickly as in autumn but will no longer be at risk from hard frosts.

Late spring: In the second and third months of spring, plant blackberries, kiwi fruit and grapevines. As young plants, these species are so sensitive to cold that they will suffer even in mild winters. You can also plant alpine and climbing strawberries at this time.

During the summer: From the end of the first month to the middle of the last month of summer, plant strawberries. The young plants are ready to form their considerably spreading rootstock during these months and will even develop the beginnings of flowerbuds.

Give the plants enough space

All plants require enough space to grow. If they are planted too close together, they will get in each other's way and prevent each other from getting enough light, sun, water and nutrients. Picking the fruit can also be tricky in confined spaces. The space between one plant and another should be large enough to accommodate the mature plants.

The right neighbours

Before planting any soft fruit plants, you should consider whether they will have suitable neighbours. This is another important factor for ensuring success when growing soft fruit.

Pollination: Pollination is not quite such an issue with soft fruit as with fruit trees. Basically, soft fruit plants are self-pollinating, so you do not really need other varieties for pollination purposes. The only exception is the hazelnut which is not self-pollinating. Experience has shown, however, that the harvest is always better if several different varieties of soft fruits are planted together, so you can kill two birds with one stone and plant early, medium-early and late varieties all in the same row. This means that you will be able to harvest the fruit for several weeks and the plants will also be pollinated more easily.

Mixed cultivation: Strawberries are highly suitable for mixed cultivation together with onions, leeks, garlic and lettuce. Onion plants, in particular, are able to protect the strawberries from fungal diseases.

Underplanting: Raspberries do very well with an underplanting that will cover the ground and protect the plants from drying out. This is very important for moisture-loving, ever-thirsty raspberries. It is a good idea to leave the soil underneath other soft fruit without plants and substitute a mulching layer to prevent drying out. The only exception is that standards can be underplanted with summer flowers or even vegetables.

NB: If the soft fruit bushes are growing in a lawn or rough grass, a circular area of bare soil, with a diameter of about 1 m (3 ft), should be left around each bush.

Planting soft fruit bushes

The planting hole: Always make sure to dig a hole that is deep enough for a soft fruit bush. Usually, young plants have not yet developed a proper rootstock, so digging the hole should not be too much of an effort. However, a little care is needed here.

● In the chosen position, dig a hole that is deep enough and a little wider than the rootstock of the plant – this will generally be about 30-50 cm (12-20 in) wide.

● Nearly all soft fruit plants have a fairly shallow, spreading root system so the hole need only be about one spade deep. Pile up the soil beside the hole.

● Loosen the soil in the hole with a garden fork by driving the fork into the soil and moving it about. Do this at intervals of about 10 cm (4 in).

● Place a little rich compost in the bottom of the hole. If the soil is very sandy, you can mix in some loam.

● Mix the soil from the hole with an equal amount of compost.

Planting: The young plant should be placed in the prepared hole and the roots spread out loosely. In the case of standard soft fruit plants, drive the support stick in beforehand. Note the correct depth of planting for different types of plants (see p. 16).

● Sprinkle the mixture of removed soil and compost over the roots.

● Make sure the soil is well distributed between the roots. If you leave large hollow spaces, the soil will later sink down and the roots will become exposed.

● When you have filled in the hole completely, press the soil down firmly by hand and give the plant plenty of water.

● Afterwards, immediately cover the soil around the plant with a layer of organic matter, such as straw, grass cuttings, dead leaves or bark mulch. Leave a little space around the neck of the roots.

Pruning when planting: Unlike fruit trees, soft fruit plants should not be pruned until after they have been planted. The reason for this is that if the young plant ends up planted deeper in the hole than it was originally in the nursery, the cut surfaces of shoots that have been removed will end up below the soil and this would create ideal conditions for the entry of germs that could cause disease. The thing to do is to delay pruning until after the soft fruit plant has been planted in its permanent position, then cut off any shoots well above the surface of the soil.

● In the case of red/white/blackcurrants and gooseberries, allow four or five of the strongest shoots to remain. These should be shortened to about half of their length. Always cut above a bud that is facing outwards.

● Jostaberries should never be pruned after planting.

● Raspberry canes should be cut back to a height of about 50 cm (20 in) to encourage young growth.

● The same goes for blackberries whose canes should be cut back to about 50 cm (20 in).

● Kiwi fruit and grapevines should not be cut back immediately after planting.

● Cutting back is not generally required for hazelnut bushes after planting but if the young plant has very long shoots they can be taken back to a length of about 30 cm (12 in) to encourage the bush to branch out.

● If you want to train an elderberry bush into a tree shape, you should allow only one strong shoot to remain standing and tie it to a stake so that it will grow straight.

Warning: Never ever cut back the roots of soft fruits when planting them!

Planting in beds

Strawberries and cranberries are generally planted in rows in a bed.

● The chosen bed should be well prepared about two weeks before planting. The soil should be loosened up and mixed with ripe compost or organic fertilizer. Fertilizer and compost should be strewn on the bed and lightly raked in, not dug in.

● The hole will be sufficient for planting if it is large enough to accommodate the rootstock.

● Bedding plants like strawberries, cranberries and blueberries will not require cutting back.

● If you want to avoid having to hoe and weed the bed, lay a black plastic mulching sheet on the bed. Hold the edges of the sheet down with soil at the edges of the bed. Cut a cross-shaped slit in the sheet for each strawberry plant and insert the young plant. The holes in the mulching sheet will allow enough water to penetrate the soil but weeds will be prevented from growing.

NB: Blueberries will only flourish in acid soil which will usually have to be created artificially in an ordinary garden environment as normal garden soil will be too alkaline to grow blueberries successfully. How to create a special "woodland" environment for growing blueberries is described on page 16.

Elderberry

This splendid elderberry tree provides a decorative screen together with wild and cultivated roses.

Planting

If you take all the plants' requirements into consideration, you should be able to count on an abundant harvest. Above all, correct planting will guarantee that the plants grow properly and quickly form new roots.
When to plant, choosing the right position and how to space soft fruit plants correctly have already been discussed on the previous pages. Now to planting itself!

Strawberries
Always plant in warm, but dull or cloudy weather to prevent the young plants from drying out.
Use a dibber to make the planting hole and place the roots vertically in the hole – strawberries root deeply.
Place the plant in the hole in such a way that the bottom of the stalks of the lowest leaves are level with the soil's surface. The heart bud should not be underground, but neither should any roots end up exposed above ground. Press down, water and place mulch around them, provided the plants have not been planted through a mulching sheet (se p. 14). If runners appear, they should be removed regularly.

Blueberries and cranberries
Dig a planting hole about one spade deep – for blueberries about 1 x 1 m (40 x 40 in); for cranberries 30 x 30 cm (12 x 12 in) per plant.
Line the hole with perforated plastic and fold the edges downwards.
Place a mixture of one third compost, one third woodland soil or bark humus and one third sedge peat in the hole, or replace compost with sand or sawdust for cranberries.
Place the young plants three fingerwidths deeper than they were in the nursery. This will encourage the formation of new shoots from the roots and, in the case of cranberries, will also ensure the formation of runners.
Water well and mulch.

Raspberries
The roots of raspberries should never be allowed to dry out during transportation. Stand the canes in water for 12 hours as soon as they arrive at your home. Plants in containers can be planted immediately. Raspberies can be planted in rows.
Prepare the bed beforehand by loosening the soil to two spades' depth and mix the top 15 cm (6 in) of soil thoroughly with rotted compost or manure (horse dung mixed with straw or sawdust is excellent). Make the planting hole deep enough so that the visible shoot buds around the neck of the rootstock are just under the soil.
Shovel soil into the hole, press down by hand (do not use your feet as this may damage the budding roots), water and immediately place a thick layer of mulch around each plant.
After pruning, tie the canes to the wires of the espalier grid.

1 Plant strawberries in such a way that the bases of the leaf stalks are just above the soil.

Red/white/blackcurrants, jostaberries and gooseberries
Loosen the soil in the planting position to about two spades' depth and remove all weeds.
Dig a planting hole about 50 x 50 cm (20 x 20 in) per plant.
Mix the soil removed from the hole with rotted compost.
Place the blackcurrant plants 10 cm (4 in) deeper than they were in the nursery. All the budding shoots should end up just below the surface of the soil to encourage the formation of new shoots from the rootstock.
Red and whitecurrants should be planted 2-3 cm (about 1 in) deeper than they were at the nursery so that about half of the shoot buds end up under the soil. In this case, new shoot formation from the rootstock is undesirable.
Jostaberries and gooseberries should be planted at the same depth as they were at the nursery.

Blackberries
Before planting, build an espalier on a house wall or make a V-shaped espalier (see illustration on p. 10). Both types of espalier are suitable for training blackberries.
Loosen the soil to two spades' depth and mix it with compost.

2 Blueberries and cranberries should be placed in a hole lined with perforated plastic sheeting.

Remove any builders' rubble over an area of at least 1 m (3 ft) and to a depth of about 50 cm (20 in) before planting if the blackberries are to be grown on an espalier along a house wall.
If you are planting in rows (on V-shaped espaliers), varieties without thorns can be set at intervals of 2 m (80 in) and varieties with thorns at intervals of 4 m (160 in).
Like raspberries, blackberries have shoot buds at the neck of the root. When planting, make sure that these buds are up to 5 cm (2 in) below the soil.
After planting, press the soil down firmly, water well and provide mulch. Then tie the branches to the espalier wires.

Grapevines

You will not need to build a support frame (a house-wall espalier usually works well, see p. 10) until the second year.
The planting hole should be dug 50 cm (20 in) from the house wall and be about two spades deep. Any builders' rubble found in the soil can be left as it will help to loosen up the soil.
Loosen the soil all around the planting hole as the roots of the grapevine tend to spread widely. Place some compost and lime in the bottom of the hole. Allow the young plant (even if it has been in a container) to stand in water for several hours before planting. Lie the plant on its side in the hole with the shoot directed towards the wall.
The grafting point should end up 5 cm (2 in) above the surface of the soil.
Fill the planting hole with soil and, after watering, heap up the soil as high as the grafting point.
Train the shoot along a stick towards the house wall. If you are planting a grapevine on a free-standing espalier or on a pergola, proceed in the same way.

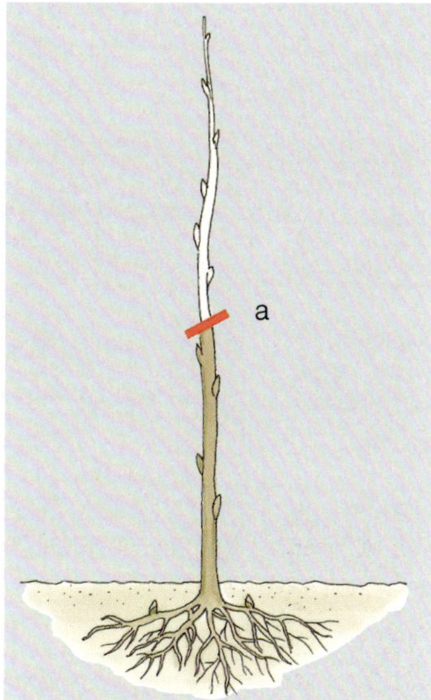

3 The root buds of raspberries should be buried 5 cm (2 in) under the ground. (a = where to cut.)

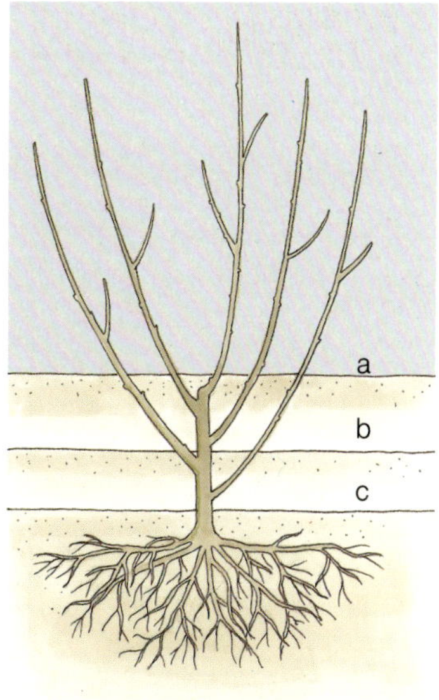

4 Planting depths: blackcurrants (a); redcurrants (b); whitecurrants (b); gooseberries and jostaberries (c).

5 A grapevine should be planted lying on its side, facing the espalier.

6 A kiwi fruit plant should sit at the same depth as before.

Kiwi fruit

Stand the rootstock, with its container, in water so that the soil becomes saturated.
Dig a planting hole about 30 cm (12 in) from the house wall or pergola. Both the diameter and the depth of the hole should be 50 cm (20 in). Loosen the soil at the bottom to one spade's depth and fill with compost. If the pH factor is more than 6, replace half of the soil removed with sedge peat as kiwi fruit plants prefer a slightly acid soil.
Place the young plant in the hole with its entire rootstock as deep as it was in its previous container.
Press down the soil, water well and immediately provide mulch.
Tie the first shoots to the support wires.

Strawberries in a herb bed
Alpine strawberries make a particularly attractive edging to a border as they flower and bear fruit from the last month of spring right through to the second month of autumn. The position should be sunny so that the fruit can develop a full flavour.
The photograph shows alpine strawberries surrounding a herb bed that has been planted with sun-loving plants like lavender, sage and nasturtiums.

Organic fertilizing and proper pruning

Good care will ensure a rich harvest

If you want permanently healthy plants and a rich harvest, there are two things you will have to make sure of: you must provide well-cared-for soil, fertilized with organic matter, and you will also need to use secateurs from time to time.

Nutrient requirements

Cultivated soft fruits are derived from wild species whose natural habitats are sunny woodland fringes or open woodland where the soil is loose, warm and full of nutrients. Here, billions of micro-organisms and other minute creatures are busily breaking down fallen leaves and decaying plant matter to supply just the right nutrients needed by the plants. The wild plant will grow only in those places where the soil meets its requirements exactly. This will rarely be the case in our gardens where the soil is worked and soil bacteria and other organisms are regularly disturbed and sometimes even destroyed. Fallen leaves and decaying plants do not often occur in a tidy garden. In addition, the plants cannot choose their own positions but are planted by us.
If you want to grow soft fruit organically, that is without recourse to chemical fertilizers and plant protection agents, you will have to try to recreate the ideal conditions of the wild.
Of course, soft fruit grown in the garden comes from cultivated plants that have been raised to produce the maximum amounts of fruit and therefore the existing nutrients in the soil will not be sufficient. The plants should be helped along with fertilizers consisting of organic matter.

Heavy soils, light soils

The type of soil you provide is extremely important if your soft fruit is to thrive. It should be loose and humus-rich, not too light but not too heavy either. Make a simple test. Take a handful of garden soil (not immediately after watering) and squeeze it in your fist. If a firm lump of soil remains in your hand when you open it again, the soil is probably heavy and full of clay. If it runs gently through your fingers when you open your hand, you are probably dealing with a very light, sandy soil. If a number of crumbly bits remain on your hand, you have friable, loose soil.
Heavy soils tend to become compacted. They do retain nutrients fairly well however, so these are not washed away into the ground water, but they are badly ventilated and will remain wet for a long time after any rainfall. In the summer, they may dry out completely and this will prevent later rain or water from penetrating the ground properly. This type of soil should be made lighter and more permeable by the addition of plenty of compost, well-rotted manure and, if necessary, some coarse sand.
Light soils usually consist mainly of sand. They are very warm, very permeable and easy to till, but water and nutrients tend to disappear downwards so that they are no longer available for the plants. Adding clay granules will help to retain water and the addition of organic matter will increase the humus content. Half-rotted compost, manure containing plenty of straw and the leaves and stems of green leguminous plants are all suitable for this purpose.
Medium soils are crumbly and loose and provide the ideal bed for all plants, including soft fruit.

Nutrients and trace elements

The organic gardener does not actually feed the plants but feeds the soil itself. This means supplying the micro-organisms in the soil with as much food as possible, which they break down into plant nutrients and trace elements. The plants will take everything they need out of the soil and there is no danger of over-fertilizing as long as you do not use large quantities of only one material, for example chicken manure. The main nutrients required by plants are nitrogen, phosphorus, potassium and calcium. The trace elements are manganese, zinc, iron, copper, magnesium, molybdenum and boron.

Nitrogen (N) is important for the growth of shoots and leaves. Nitrogen deficiency shows up in lack of growth, yellow leaves, malformation of buds and small or no fruit. Overfertilizing with nitrogen causes overproduction of shoots and leaves, watery, tasteless fruit, scab and severe infestation with aphids.

Phosphorus (P) is important for the growth of roots and for the formation of flowerbuds, which means a good harvest. Phosporus deficiency hardly ever occurs in gardens.

Potassium (K) helps to make the plants resistant to pests, diseases and frost and regulates the amount and use of fluids and the storage of nutrients. In plants with potassium deficiency, the leaves drop early and the fruit is tasteless. An excess of potassium means that the plant cannot absorb enough calcium and magnesium and the formation of fruit ceases.

Calcium (Ca) is an important nutrient in the soil. It enables the plant to absorb nutrients but also encourages the proliferation of micro-organisms in the soil. A soil deficient in calcium means that it has a low pH factor and that it is acid. A large amount of calcium in the soil yields pH values above 7 which means the soil is alkaline.

Magnesium (Mg) is important for the formation of chlorophyll in the leaves of plants. This, in turn, is necessary for the production of food from sunlight through photosynthesis.

Trace elements are only absorbed in minute quantities but if they are lacking signs of deficiency will become apparent. For example, raspberries often suffer from iron dificiency, causing the leaves to turn yellow and the plant to wither.

Herbal brews and other home-made liquid fertilizers

Herbal brews

Fresh nettles (always pick them before the seeds have formed), borage, rhubarb or cabbage leaves and other herbs should be sliced into 10 cm (4 in) long strips (see also p. 22). Half-fill a plastic or wooden bucket (never a metal bucket!) with the cut leaves and fill to 10 cm (4 in) below the rim with rainwater. Stand the container in the sun where fermentation will begin after about 24 hours. Stir once daily. The brew will be ready to use when the plant matter sinks to the bottom.

Pour the brew around the roots of plants in a ratio of 1 litre (1¾ pt) of brew to 10 litres (17½ pt) of water.

Compost brew

Add one shovelful of well-rotted compost to 10 litres (17½ pt) of water and stir well. Pour the liquid around the roots of plants.

Liquid fertilizer made out of organic ready-to-use fertilizer

Add two handfuls of a horn-blood-bonemeal mixture to one large watering can. Fill the can with water and stir thoroughly several times. Pour the undiluted mixture around the roots of the plants.

What to use as fertilizer

Garden compost contains all the main nutrients and many trace elements. In addition, it also contains soil bacteria which are vital to the maintenance of healthy soil. As a rule, therefore, always give your soft fruit plants compost in early spring, placing it around the roots of bushes and in between the rows of leafy soft fruit plants. Compost should only be raked in superficially on the surface, never dug in.

Animal manure should only be used if it is well rotted; that is, if earthworms have begun to invade it and it smells pleasantly of fresh soil. Even then, a 5 cm (2 in) thick layer will be quite sufficient in the spring. Blueberries and cranberries should never be given manure.

Organic fertilizer is on sale in the gardening trade in various forms. It should be mixed with the same amount of compost and strewn around the plants' roots, following the manufacturers' instructions meticulously.

Horn-blood-bonemeal mix is an organic fertilizer which can be added to soft fruit plants as early as the last month of winter. If you have discovered that there is an excess of phosphates in your garden you should use hornmeal alone, as blood and bonemeal contain phosphates. These preparations can also be sprinkled in the planting hole – following the manufacturer's instructions very carefully!

Lime (calcium) is required by most soft fruit plants but care should be taken when using it. First, test the pH factor of your soil using an indicator stick and target only those areas that need lime. Most soft fruit plants require soil with a pH value between 5 and 6.5 which is slightly acid.

Cultivated blueberries like very acid soils with a pH value of 4-5; cranberries prefer 5-6; grapevines prefer a slightly alkaline soil with a value of 6-7.
Mulching matter can also provide some fertilizer but is mainly used for covering the soil. If you use fresh plant debris for mulching (weeds that have been pulled up, stinging nettles, borage, vegetable leaves, etc.), they will have a slight fertilizing effect. If you use straw for mulching, you will have to add a nitrogen-rich fertilizer (horn chips, horse manure, guano), as a lot of nitrogen is used up by decomposing straw.

Brews and fermented liquids as additional fertilizer

An alternative to organic fertilizers that can be bought is fermented plant brews which you can make yourself (see p. 21). On their own they will not produce a sufficient quantity of nutrients for all types of soil but they are important additional forms of fertilizer when used along with compost and organic fertilizers. They can also be employed any time you notice that plants are not growing properly and may be suffering from lack of nutrients.
Liquid fertilizer can also be produced from most organic ready-made fertilizers. These are particularly good for shallow-rooted soft fruit plants. Solid fertilizers have to be worked into the soil, which often damages the roots of the bushes.
Fermented nettle brew contains nitrogen, magnesium and trace elements.
Fermented borage brew contains nitrogen and a lot of potassium (important for raspberries).
Fermented brews made from cabbage leaves, onions and garlic fortified with plants like chamomile, dandelion and lemon balm are not only good as additional fertilizers, they are also important for ensuring the health of the plant and the soil.
Fermented rhubarb leaf brew contains nitrogen and oxalic acid which fortify the plant tissues.
Compost brew is a fast cure for soft fruits that are not producing enough fruit. It appears to work immediately on leafy soft fruit plants and at the very latest in the following year on bushes or canes.
NB: Most organic fertilizers do not work immediately as they are long-term fertilizers. Fermented herbal brews do ensure rapid improvement but are "gentle" fertilizers that will not cause radical interference in the structure of the plant.

When to fertilize

During the autumn, add half-rotted compost, grass cuttings or other fresh garden refuse as mulch around the bushes or use other durable mulching matter. This mulching layer may rot during the winter and early spring and so will not produce nutrients but these would not be needed during the winter anyway. If you were to give the plants active fertilizer during this time of year, the nutrients would only end up being washed away into the ground water.
In early spring, or even around the end of the last month of winter, remove the mulching layer so that the soil can warm up faster. Add ripe compost or well-rotted manure to all soft fruit plants. In addition to the compost or manure, sprinkle organic fertilizers like a horn-blood-bonemeal mix or something similar – you can even obtain special organic soft fruit fertilizers in the gardening trade.
After flowering, use fermented herbal brews for the first time. These can be given to all soft fruit – except strawberries – up to four weeks before the fruit is ripe. Vigorously growing or heavily cropping bushes (for example, kiwi fruit) are very grateful for a boost from these herbal brews.
After the harvest, it is only strawberries that will need a good dose of ripe compost as they are now producing the beginnings of flowerbuds for the following year.

Watering

Soft fruits require plenty of water. Most of them are shallow-rooting plants, which means that the roots spread rather than grow deep. If it has not rained for a long time, the plant becomes very thirsty and the fruit will turn out small and sometimes even be quite dry. Strawberries have deep-growing roots but their abundant foliage means that they lose a lot of moisture through evaporation. Soft fruits growing against house walls never receive enough water through rainfall, even in wet weather. With the exception of cranberries, which like dry, poor soils, all other soft fruits require a position where the soil is unable to dry out quickly. This creates a dilemma for the gardener as, on the one hand, soft fruits like a warm, sunny position but, on the other hand, the soil is supposed to remain moist. The solution is mulching (see p. 14). If there is a thick layer of mulch under soft fruit plants, this will help to retain moisture in the soil and there is no need to keep on watering.

A strawberry barrel needs a sunny position.

Pruning

Soft fruit bushes have to be pruned from time to time. Firstly, this helps to thin them out so that the fruits inside the bushes can obtain enough light. Secondly, pruning encourages rejuvenation and the best fruits grow on the younger shoots. Most soft fruit plants are pruned after the harvest or during the winter. You will only need to use your secateurs occasionally during the summer.

Strawberries
(illustration 1)
Regularly cut off all runners that are not going to be utilized for propagation (see p. 32). This will enable the plant to put all its energy into the production of fruit. After harvesting the crop of large fruit varieties, cut off all the leaves apart from the heart.
Alpine strawberries and ground-covering strawberries should be cut back radically after harvesting; use the lawn mower on plants that cover large areas. Very often these plants will produce a second crop later in the year. Do not cut back climbing strawberries.

1 The outer leaves of strawberries should be removed after the harvest.

Red/white/blackcurrants
(illustration 2)
After harvesting or during the winter after the leaves have fallen, cut off all older shoots (dark stems) near the ground or just above the point where the young shoot grows. Also remove any weak shoots or those growing towards the centre. You should be left with eight to ten strong new shoots.
In the case of standards, also cut out old shoots and shorten any shoots that are too long.

Gooseberries
(illustration 3)
Cut out any old wood near the base so that you are left with about 10-12 strong, outward-growing shoots. During the winter, shorten all of the shoots of varieties susceptible to attack by mildew by about 10 cm (4 in).

Jostaberries
From the fourth year after planting, cut out the oldest branches and shoots. Leave the medium-strong shoots as they will bear more fruit than the stronger ones. Shorten any shoots that are too long, or hang down to the ground, by about half.

Raspberries
(illustration 4)
Cut back the old canes that have borne fruit during the summer to just above the ground. Allow only about ten of the strongest young shoots to remain standing to provide next year's harvest.
NB: If you are growing autumn raspberries, cut off all the canes close to the ground during the autumn. The young shoots of this variety will not start growing until the spring.

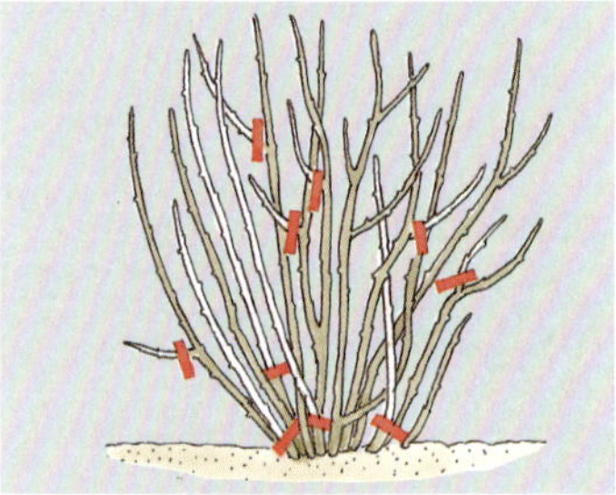

2 Allow about eight to ten vigorous young shoots to remain.

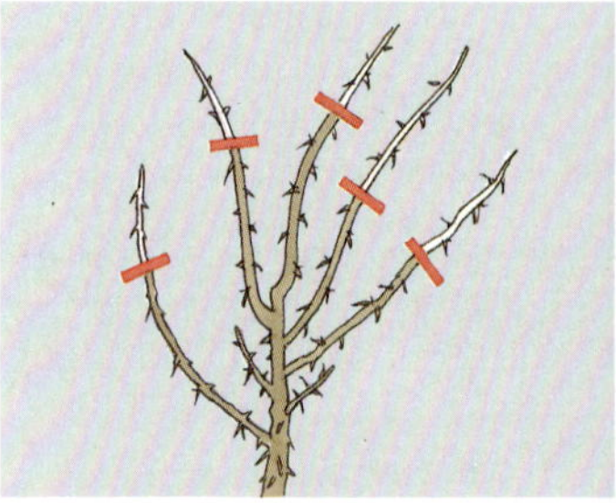

3 Shorten the shoots of gooseberries in the winter.

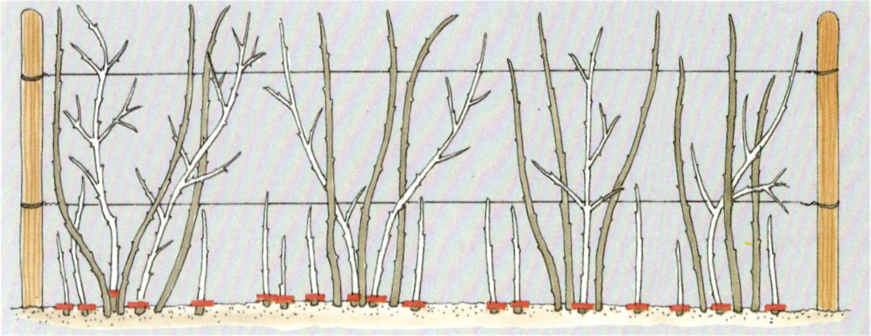

4 The old raspberry canes should be cut off near the ground as soon as the harvest is over.

Grapevines
(illustration 5)
This illustration shows how to do summer pruning. Before this, however, other forms of pruning should also have been carried out.
Around the end of the last month of winter/first month of spring, cut off the young shoots that formed the previous summer, leaving only two or three buds. The uppermost bud should point outwards, away from the main shoot. Allow a stump of about 2 cm (¾ in) to remain above this bud to prevent it from drying out. New shoots will grow out of these buds.
At the beginning of the first month of summer, cut out any shoots that are packed too close together, and also any suckers on the old wood.
Leave only two young shoots with flowerbuds on each shoot stump.
Summer pruning (see illustration) involves cutting back all potential fruit-bearing shoots, above the outer inflorescences, to two leaves as soon as the fruit is about pea-size. The remaining shoots in the leaf axils should be cut back to one leaf.

Kiwi fruit
(illustration 6)
During the winter, cut off all shoots that have previously borne fruit. When the fruit has attained walnut-size, during the second or third month of summer, cut off all shoots at the sixth leaf above the last fruit.
If you have plenty of room on a house wall or pergola, you can allow kiwi plants to grow without cutting them back, as they will still yield a good crop of fruit.

5 With grapevines, cut back the fruit-bearing shoots after they have flowered in the summer.

6 From the first month of summer onwards, shorten the fruit-bearing shoots of kiwi fruit plants.

Blackberries
(illustration 7)
During the summer, cut back the shoots in the leaf axils to leave four buds (the new fruit-bearing shoots will grow out of these).
During the winter, cut off all the old branches (light-coloured in the illustration) at ground level. Tie up four to eight young shoots so they are evenly spaced out. In very cold regions, lie them on the ground and cover them with straw.

Elderberries
As a rule, cutting back will not be necessary. Only if you want to harvest particularly large berries should you need to rejuvenate the tree by regular pruning.
Rejuvenating involves cutting back all older branches and all branches growing inwards. If the tree or bush becomes too large and does not bear much fruit, cut it back severely to 50 cm (20 in). Two years after doing this, it will produce a rich harvest of fruit again.

Hazelnuts
Any shoots growing up from the rootstock should be cut off every summer or in the autumn at the very latest. An old hazel bush should be cut back severely to a height of 50 cm (20 in) every 15 years. Allow only three new shoots to remain on these pruned branches.

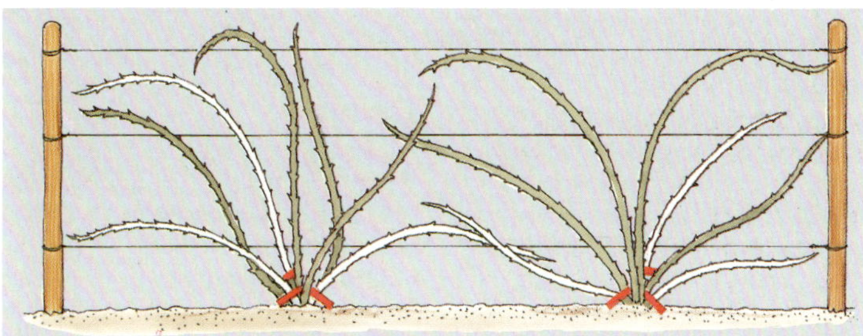

7 Cut off old blackberry canes just above the ground in winter. For each bush, tie up four to eight young canes, well spaced out.

A rich berry harvest on a patio

Even if you do not have a garden you need not give up the idea of growing your own soft fruit. Some plants can be grown quite easily in large containers, although plants in pots will require more care and attention than those grown in the garden. The following section explains how to obtain a successful harvest even in a very small space.

Strawberries, red/white/ blackcurrants, gooseberries, jostaberries, blueberries, grapevines and even kiwi fruit can be cultivated in large containers without too much trouble. Soft fruit plants in pots may take various different forms. Elegant standards, for example, can be made out of red/white/ blackcurrants, gooseberries and jostaberries in large containers. These plants would spread too much if they were grown as bushes. Grapevines and kiwi fruit can be allowed to climb along a balcony railing. Even blueberry plants can be grown in large containers and the specially developed low-growing varieties are ideal for cultivation in pots. Raspberries can be grown to screen off a neighbouring balcony. They will have to be planted in a wide, long container for this purpose. Strawberries can be grown in a number of different ways on patios or balconies, for example in hanging containers, in pots on trellises, in a strawberry barrel, in a bed cut into a wall or pillar.

Think of the weight!

Before purchasing container plants, you should give some thought to the final weight of the fully grown fruit-bearing plants on your balcony or roof garden. The plant itself is only one part of this weight. The weight of the container with its load of damp soil also needs to be considered. Remember that, after watering, the weight of the container will increase by about half again. The average extra weight that is safe on modern balconies or roof gardens is generally in the range of 250 kg (550 lb) per square metre. Do not forget to allow for the weight of the existing floor covering, like tiles. In the case of older buildings with balconies or patios that have been added later on, it is a good idea to consult a structural engineer or, if possible, look at the original plans.

Large containers

The size of the container is important. Soft fruit plants should never be planted in containers that are too small for them. A standard soft fruit plant will require a pot with a diameter of at least 40-50 cm (16-20 in) for the first few years. Grapevines and kiwi fruit will require a much larger pot with a capacity of about 100 litres (22 gal) if the plant is to grow strong and healthy. Raspberries are best grown in deep, wide and very heavy boxes standing on the ground. A large flowerpot will be sufficient for strawberries and the pot varieties of blueberries.

The material out of which the containers are made is not quite so important for the well-being of the plants. Clay pots are very decorative but are also heavy and water evaporates rather quickly through this porous material. Large plastic containers are easier to transport and will keep the soil moist but they do not look as nice. Deft do-it-yourselfers may be able to disguise plastic pots by covering them with a suitable surface material. Or the plastic pots can be painted in bright colours using environmentally friendly acrylic varnish. Large containers often come equipped with too few drainage holes, so use a wood drill to make extra holes in the bottom. Concrete containers are best for raspberries as the canes can easily tip over in less weighty containers.

The right soil

Soft fruit plants in large containers cannot spread their roots far into the ground so, right from the start, you must make provision for an adequate supply of nutrients and water. The soil must allow water to permeate throughout without becoming compact or acid. The best basic mixture for soft fruits grown in containers is half humus-rich garden soil and half compost. If your garden soil is very light and sandy, you will have

Even when grown in a balcony tub, strawberry plants will produce juicy fruit.

to add a little loam. Also add a handful of ground charcoal, a shovelful of sand per container and some controlled-release organic fertilizer (follow the manufacturer's instructions as to the amount to use). All of this should be thoroughly mixed together and used as it is, without sieving it, as the larger pieces in the mixture will prevent the compost from becoming compacted. If you are growing soft fruit in only one pot, you can use flower compost instead, which can be mixed with a little sand or, even better, with fine gravel.

Buying and planting

Make sure that the varieties you have chosen are particularly suitable for growing in large containers. Always check that the fine roots are well developed.

My tip: When buying standards, make sure that they have a crown that is at least one year old. For raspberries, choose varieties that bear fruit from the second month of summer until the middle of autumn and which do not have to be cut back until late autumn.

How to plant

- First, lay a 10 cm (4 in) thick layer of gravel in the container to provide good drainage.
- Add some soil on top of this.
- Set the plant in the container so that the roots are well spread out.
- Always stand the support stake right beside a standard's stem.
- Add the rest of the soil, making sure that all hollow spaces between the roots are filled.
- The root buds should be covered with soil.
- In the case of grapevines, make sure the grafting point is exposed.
- When all of the soil has been inserted, press it down to form a watering "gulley" around the edge of the container and water well.

Care

Soft fruit plants grown in large containers will generally require a little more care and attention than those grown in the garden.

Watering

Freshly planted soft fruit plants should be kept only slightly moist. Once the plants have become established, however, they will require relatively large amounts of water. The best plan is to water regularly in the evenings with water that has been allowed to stand all day. Covering the soil with large chunks of gravel will prevent the moisture from evaporating too quickly.

Fertilizing

Fertilizing will hardly be necessary during the first year as sufficient nutrients should be contained in the soil or compost. Potted plants can also be given fermented herbal brews from time to time. From the second year onwards, however, some of the nutrients in the compost will have been used up and it will become necessary to fertilize the plants. Use liquid organic fertilizer in early spring, then, if possible, fermented herbal brews every two weeks and one dose of compost brew after flowering. If you are unable to prepare any fermented herbal brews or compost brew, you will have to give the plants organic fertilizer every four weeks.

My tip: Mix two handfuls of horn-blood-bonemeal compound in a bucket of water and allow it to stand in a secluded corner of the balcony. This liquid fertilizer is excellent for feeding to your soft fruit plants.

Pruning

Standards in pots should be cut back in the autumn to prevent the crown from bending over too far and possibly snapping off. This will also encourage the cut shoots to branch out better. The crown should be thinned out every year if you want to obtain abundant crops of fruit. Strawberries in pots should be cut back after the harvest is finished and, in the case of varieties with large fruits, runners should be removed on a regular basis. After two years, these plants should be replaced with new ones.

Thinning out

Thinning out the fruit may also be necessary, particularly with gooseberries. If the prospective crop is abundant, remove half of the fruit while it is still half ripe. It can be used for making jam or flans. Thinning out prevents the weaker branches from breaking off under the weight of the fruit and the remaining fruit will grow particularly large and sweet.

Repotting

Even with the best fertilizing, no plants can remain in the same containers for years on end. Every two to three years, soft fruit plants will need repotting. Remove the plant from the container, shake off the soil or compost, which should fall out of the roots by itself, and then return the plant to the pot with fresh soil or compost. Avoid damaging the roots in any way. Climbing plants cannot be removed from a container. Instead, add a layer of compost on top every year. If you cannot make your own compost, you can buy ready-made varieties by the sackful.

Overwintering

As a rule, soft fruit plants are hardy but if they are grown in containers or pots they are more at risk during the cold season of the year. In large containers, the roots are particularly at risk in frosty weather as frost will tend to freeze the compost or soil so that the roots receive no moisture.

- The safest plan is to overwinter soft fruit plants in a greenhouse or conservatory or in a bright, cool room. Here, soft fruit plants can be treated like other large container plants during the cold season.
- If the plants are standing on a patio or balcony, pack the container in several layers of newspaper and add insulating bubble pack on the outside. Even a jute sack filled with dead leaves and straw may provide some protection. During the winter months, check often to see whether the soil is still moist. If not, water a little but only on mild days.
- Strawberry barrels, kiwi fruit and grapevines can be protected with conifer branches or reed mats which will also shield them against the harsh winter sunlight which can cause a lot of damage as it may thaw out frozen plant cells much too fast, causing the cell walls to burst. The results are cracks in the bark, dying buds and decaying leaves.

Plant protection on patios and balconies

Pests and diseases tend to occur more often among plants on patios and balconies than among those in the garden. The reasons for this are that pests are not destroyed so readily by useful insects in these positions as they would be in the garden; the balcony may suffer from stagnant air or draughts; and aphids may transfer from other balcony and large container plants. Fungal infections are encouraged by lack

of ventilation during humid weather. Pests and diseases that are common to certain species of plant should be controlled in the same way as for soft fruits in the garden (see pp. 34-9).
To discourage fungal infections, spray the plants as early as spring, at intervals of four to six weeks, with mare's tail brew, remembering also to spray the surface of the soil underneath the plants. Aphids and other harmful insects can be eliminated quite easily with simple, natural substances. Sticky insect tags, as used for indoor and greenhouse plants, should get rid of invading insects.

Soft fruits for decorating patios and balconies
Soft fruit plants make excellent decorative features on patios or balconies

- Raspberries, for example, are ideal as an attractive boundary between neighbouring balconies. They will have to be tied up properly, however, preferably to wires that pass in front of and behind the canes to prevent them from falling over.
- Grapevines and kiwi fruit may be trained all round the balcony, but will require a stable supporting grid as the fruits are quite heavy. You could even build a kind of pergola to create a bower on a protruding balcony and train the plant over this. If another balcony is positioned above your own, you can train the creepers along the underside of this upper balcony but only along the outside edge as the inside edge would be too dark for the fruit to develop.
- A strawberry barrel (see p. 11) can be placed on a large balcony, a roof garden or a patio.

A tayberry standard (a cross between a raspberry and a blackberry).

Raising your own soft fruits

Most soft fruit plants are easy to propagate but it is only the propagation of young strawberry and raspberry plants that is really worth the effort. In the case of other types of soft fruit, you can buy new plants very inexpensively and they are usually guaranteed to be free of disease.

Use healthy varieties

As a rule, soft fruit plants are quite robust and not very susceptible to disease but certain diseases can be passed on via propagation, such as root rot in strawberries and various viral diseases among soft fruit bushes. Sometimes an individual variety may be particularly susceptible to certain diseases, for example to American gooseberry mildew. Try to avoid propagating from these varieties. If you are not really certain that your own soft fruit plants are absolutely healthy and disease-resistant you should not experiment with propagating. There are plenty of virus-tested plants and disease-resistant varieties to be bought in the gardening trade.

Why soft fruit plants are grafted

Occasionally, your own home-propagated soft fruit plants may not produce any fruit at all. Some soft fruits, for example grapevines, kiwi fruit and certain varieties of red/white/blackcurrants, have to be grafted on to a stock. This is necessary because either the scions do not root well or not at all or because the plants can only be propagated as pure varieties in this way.
When propagating seedlings, for example in the case of kiwi fruit, you will often obtain "crossbreeds" which bear hardly any fruit or none at all.
Another reason for grafting is that a robust stock and rooting system are required for a delicate variety. In the case of grapevines, grafting is done because only those vines that are resistant to the vine pest *Phylloxera* can be planted and the best way to ensure this is by grafting. If you have green fingers and some experience with grafting fruit trees, you may wish to have a go at grafting soft fruit. Stocks are not easy to come by and the grafting of the very slender shoots of soft fruits is a complicated procedure, however, so it is generally not worth the trouble for the layperson.

Which soft fruit to propagate

Soft fruit plants can be propagated in various different ways but the following methods are the most suitable. (See also pp. 32 and 33.)
Strawberries are propagated from the young plantlets growing on the runners. Alpine strawberries are sown in flat trays in the first and second months of spring and can be grown initially on a windowsill or in a greenhouse until they have formed adequate roots. Then plant them outside.
Red/white/blackcurrants can be propagated from cuttings or by layering shoots that hang down to the ground. Blackcurrants, in particular, can be propagated quite easily by layering and will even propagate this way by themselves. Among redcurrants there are some varieties whose shoots cannot be propagated in this way (for example "Heinemann's Rote Spätlese"). These varieties are grafted on to jostaberry stocks in tree nurseries.
Gooseberries can be propagated from cuttings or hanging shoots.

The first proper harvest

blackberries	4 years
blueberries	3-4 years
cranberries	2 years
currants	
red, white	3 years
black	2 years
elderberries	4 years
gooseberries	2 years
grapevines	3 years
hazelnut	5 years
jostaberries	3 years
kiwi fruit	5 years
raspberries (autumn)	same year
raspberries (summer)	1 year
strawberries	1 year

Gooseberries prefer loamy, nutrient-rich, alkaline soil.

Jostaberries are easy to propagate from downward-hanging shoots and cuttings.

Raspberries produce young canes from their roots during the summer, but at the same time also produce long underground suckers. The plants that grow from these are used for propagation. When cutting them out, make sure that the roots of the remaining young canes are not damaged.

Blackberries can be propagated from downward-hanging laterals or by taking a cutting from an entire cane. The cane will produce young plants in several places.

Blueberries can be propagated from downward-hanging laterals during the last month of spring or by using shoot tips that are cut during the summer and rooted in pots. This method will not always work so it is a good idea to buy additional young plants.

Cultivated cranberries form tiny plantlets on their runners, which can be planted in a new bed during the spring.

Grapevines are better grafted. This is very complicated for the layperson so it is probably better to buy new young vines.

Hazelnuts propagate from their own nut kernels in the wild. The cultivated varieties have been grafted, however, and must be bought.

Elderberry is one of the soft fruits that are best bought as young plants. You may find young elderberry plants all around your garden but it will take years until these seedlings bear fruit.

Kiwi fruits are grafted on to robust stocks of the genus *Actinidia*. Propagation from seed is rarely successful.

NB: Standards of gooseberries, red/white/blackcurrants and jostaberries have been grafted on to *Ribes* stock just below the crown.

Propagating

There are many different methods of propagating plants. The following are the most suitable for various types of soft fruit and are therefore most likely to be successful. I shall not dwell on grafting, however, as this method should, as a rule, be left to the experts (see p. 30).

Cuttings

Strawberries

Mark the healthiest-looking and most abundant fruit-bearing strawberry plants in your bed. During the second month of summer the plants will produce plenty of runners which, in turn, will each form several little strawberry plants. To propagate, proceed as follows. Fill a peat propagation pot with compost. Place the young plant that is growing nearest to your chosen parent plant in the pot but do not separate it from the parent plant. Cut off the rest of the shoot. A good rootstock should have formed within about four weeks' time. Now cut off the runner and plant the young plant in a bed. If you require lots of cuttings, this method will be too time-consuming. In that case, cut off the shoots nearest to the plant even if they have only a few roots. First plant them in flowerpots in seedling compost. As soon as they have developed good rootstocks, they can be transferred to a bed.

Seed

Alpine strawberries

Sow the seed in dishes containing seeding compost during the first month of spring and stand them in a warm position. About six weeks later, prick out the seedlings and put them in small peat pots filled with seedling compost or lightly fertilized flower compost. Leave them in a warm position until a good rootstock has developed. Water regularly. As soon as strong young plants have formed (about the middle of the last month of spring) you can plant them outside.

Alternatively, alpine strawberries can also be sown in an early bed around the last month of spring or first month of summer. They should be pricked out several times and then placed in their permanent position during the first month of autumn. They can be overwintered here if they are protected with a covering of conifer branches.

Layering lateral shoots

Red/white/blackcurrants, gooseberries, blackberries, raspberries

Do this in early summer.

At the place where you intend to push a lateral shoot into the soil, the soil should be humus-rich but not fertilized too much. Loosen the soil and mix it with compost and a little sand.

Choose vigorous, one- or two-year-old shoots and remove their flowers and fruit. The shoots should be bent downwards to the ground and then anchored with a piece of bent wire about 20 cm (8 in) below the tip of the shoot so that the shoot is lying right on the ground. It is a good idea to place a little soil on the anchoring point. The part which is lying on the soil or is covered with soil must have buds as it is from these that the roots and new shoots will grow. By the following early summer, when roots and new shoots have formed, the young plant can be separated from the parent plant and planted in its own position.

Another method is suitable for blackberries and raspberries. From the second month of summer onwards, a one-year-old cane can be laid in the soil along its entire length without separating it from the parent plant.

1 Strawberries form runners. Plant the young plantlets nearest to the parent in pots and separate them after about four weeks.

2 Sow alpine strawberries in trays from the first month of spring onwards, prick out the seedlings and plant out from the last month of spring.

3 When layering, downward-hanging laterals should be firmly anchored at the points where they are meant to form roots.

4 Raspberries produce young plants from suckers during the first month of summer. These can be separated in the autumn.

Anchor it in one or two places with pieces of bent wire or weigh it down with stones and cover it with a thin layer of soil. Young plants will grow from nearly all the buds.
After about a year, separate it from the parent plant and move it to the desired position.

Suckers
Raspberries
During the first month of summer, raspberries produce young canes from suckers that grow beside the main canes. These can be removed during the first month of autumn or in the following spring. Suckers bearing young plants about 1 metre (40 in) tall can be lifted slightly with the help of a garden fork so that the roots are exposed.
Make sure that one or two root buds are visible on the roots of the young canes. Use these canes only.
Selected young plants can be separated from the sucker with secateurs. Immediately plant the young canes in the chosen position.

Cuttings
Red/white/blackcurrants, gooseberries, jostaberries
Prepare a bed with loosened soil that has been mixed with a little sand. The cuttings can stand close together to begin with so they will not need a lot of room. During the first and second months of spring, cut one-year-old shoots into about 20 cm (8 in) long sections.
The cut at the lower end should always be made just below a bud. Place the cuttings close together in the prepared bed so that only one or two buds are exposed above ground.

5 Currants, jostaberries and gooseberries can be propagated from cuttings.

The cuttings will form roots during the course of a year and also produce one or two shoots. Remove these one-year-old plants from the soil and shorten the new shoots by about a third so that they will branch out better.
Plant the cuttings in a larger bed at intervals of about 30-50 cm (12-20 in).
You will have ready-to-plant young plants by the following autumn.

Tips on care
Cuttings and plants from suckers should be watered regularly after replanting. Weeds should be removed. Cuttings and layered, rooted lateral shoots also require care. In periods of drought, make sure that the soil is kept constantly moist.

Plant protection

Healthy fruit without chemicals

Soft fruits are intended for human consumption. For this reason you should avoid the use of toxic sprays to control pests and diseases in your garden. If you take all the right preventive measures and, when needed, use only mechanical or biological means, you can avoid using

Biological plant protection means sticking mainly to nature's own rules and making use of them in the right way. The balance of nature should not be tampered with or altered in any way.

Proper care

- Not all varieties of soft fruit are suitable for any climate.
- The soil should be loose and nutrient-rich.
- The soil should always be covered with a layer of mulch.
- The position should be sunny and preferably in shade for only a few hours per day. It should also be sheltered from the wind.
- The plants should never be grown too close together.
- Bushes should be given plenty of air and sunlight in their centres by thinning them out every year, otherwise they risk attack by fungal infections.
- Ensure that plants receive sufficient nourishment by using compost and other organic fertilizers.
- Plants which secrete special substances from their roots and leaves, which ward off pests and promote the healthy growth of neighbouring plants, should be planted in the immediate vicinity of soft fruit plants.

The right neighbours

Mixed cultivation: Strawberries, in particular, may benefit from mixed cultivation. Garlic, onions or leeks planted between the rows act as a preventive against fungal diseases. Spinach, lettuce and borage encourage growth.

Underplanting: Red/white/blackcurrants can be protected from rust with an underplanting of wormwood. Dwarf beans growing under raspberries collect and store nitrogen and their leaves should be left to rot in situ. An underplanting of marigold (*Calendula*) keeps the soil healthy.

Good neighbours: Blackcurrants tend to flourish particularly well in the vicinity of bitter cherries. Gooseberries and red/white/blackcurrants planted alternately appear to promote each other's well-being.

Individual planting: Grapevines and kiwi fruit like to stand on their own. Blueberries and cranberries prefer very acid soil, which other plants do not like, so avoid a mixed cultivation here.

Avoid competition: At the other end of the scale are competitive plants like grasses and weeds which will compete with soft fruit for water and nutrients. The dense roots of a very nutrient-hungry lawn are tough competition, particularly for shallow-rooting plants. The same goes for weeds, particularly ground elder (*Aegopodium podagraria*), *Convolvulus* and couch grass. The soil around the roots of soft fruit should always be kept free of weeds.

My tip: Suppression of competitive plants can be achieved by a very simple but effective method. Lay well-rotted compost or strew organic fertilizer and a little lime around the roots of the bushes (except raspberry canes) in early spring. On top, lay cardboard, newspapers and, finally, a layer of straw. This covering is permeable so the bushes will still obtain enough water but the lack of light underneath it will ensure that any competitive plants are eliminated after about two years.

Preventive measures against pests and diseases

You can still take preventive measures against harmful predators and even against fungal infections without any kind of chemical spraying.

Useful insects

Useful insects are some of the most effective helpers of the soft fruit gardener. If you can protect them or even ensure that they are introduced to the garden, pests will never have a chance to gain the upperhand.

Mixed cultivation: *onions or leeks planted between the rows as a preventive against fungal infections.*

Ladybirds, lacewings, earwigs, predatory mites, hoverflies, ichneumon flies, beetles and and spiders prey primarily on harmful insects.

Protect the useful insects by refusing to use any chemical insecticides. These agents will almost certainly kill such helpful insects while still only temporarily eliminating pests. The harmful insects live on plants; the useful insects live exclusively on harmful insects. If you use chemical sprays, the pests will rapidly multiply again but no useful insects will be left to control them. If you use biological insecticides which leave useful insects unharmed (for example, when pests have taken over to such a degree that the useful insects can no longer cope with the situation), you should make sure that only about two thirds of the pests are destroyed. If the useful insects have no more pests to feed on, they will move on or die of hunger.

Support your helpful insects by growing plenty of flowering plants around your soft fruit plants. Adult hoverflies and lacewings, for example, live on flower nectar and pollen, while their larvae consume huge quantities of pests. Providing winter quarters for useful insects will also encourage them to stay. Try lacewing boxes (see p. 36), old pieces of wood with holes bored in them and old pieces of tree stump. Do not tidy up the garden too meticulously in the autumn; leave some dead leaves and withered plants in the flowerbeds.

Mechanical control

Mechanical measures of protection are some of the oldest methods of keeping pests and diseases at bay in the garden. One of the best bird deterrents is still a scarecrow but sticky rings, snail fences, nets and plastic sheets can also be helpful. (See pp. 38 and 39.)

Controling fungal infections

Mildew, grey mould, rust and scab are fungal infestations. Strawberries and grapevines are particularly at risk. If a plant is already badly infested, neither biological preparations nor chemical sprays will help. Plant brews should be employed prophylactically against fungal infections. Spray plants and soil every three weeks from early spring until four weeks before harvest (for strawberries, again from late summer).

Making your own sprays

Tansy brew: for controlling mites and as a preventive measure against infestation with mildew and rust. Mix 300 g (10½ oz) tansy with 10 litres (17½ pt) of water. After one week, dilute 1:2 with water and use for spraying plants.

Mare's tail brew: as a preventive against fungal infections.
Place 1 kg (2 lb 3 oz) fresh mare's tail (chopped) or 150 g (5 oz) dried leaves in water and leave overnight. Next day, simmer for about 30 minutes. After it has cooled, strain it and spray leaves and soil with diluted liquid (1:5).

Nettle brew: for controlling caterpillars and aphids.
Soak fresh nettles in water for 24 hours. Spray undiluted.

Quassia brew: for all pests. Soak 150 g (5 oz) quassia compound (from chemists) in 2 litres (3½ pt) of water for 24 hours then boil for one hour. After cooling, dilute with 10 litres (17½ pt) of water and use as a spray. **Warning:** This will also kill useful insects!

Soft soap solution: for control of aphids and caterpillars.
Dilute 1 cup of soft soap (better still, use special plant soap) in 10 litres (17½ pt) of water. Do not spray on ripe berries – it tastes horrible!

Pests and diseases of raspberries, blackberries and strawberries	
	***Raspberry cane disease:*** Violet-coloured spots on young canes, flaking bark. Prevention: Healthy plants can be sprayed with tansy brew at the beginning of the third month of spring; mulch around the plants; plant marigolds (*Calendula*). Control: immediately remove infested canes and destroy them. Grow new canes in a different position.
	***Blackberry gall mite:*** The fruit has red spots or is completely red and remains hard. Prevention: Spray soil and plants with tansy brew after pruning in the autumn. Control: Cut off infested canes and burn them.
	***Root rot (strawberries):*** The plants look sickly, leaves wither, leaves and roots show reddish discoloration. Prevention: Buy healthy plants (see p. 12); do not overfertilize. Change the bed every three to four years. Control: Destroy infested plants.
	***Strawberry mildew:*** Undersides of leaves are reddish, with a fine, white film. The leaves roll up, the fruit remains small, hard and inedible. Prevention: Mare's tail brew or other agents as for grey mould; grow resistant varieties. Control: Destroy infested plants.
	***Grey mould (strawberries):*** Berries are covered in thick grey mould. Prevention: Space out plants; do not provide too much nitrogen in spring; do not water in the evenings. In late summer and from early spring onwards, spray with mare's tail brew etc. to prevent fungal infections. Control: Remove any infested fruit.

Methods of control

When pests and diseases appear, immediate action is called for if you want to avoid endangering the entire harvest.

Cutting and removing: In the early stages of infestation, disease may be combated by severe cutting away of infested parts of plants. This is especially important with fungal infections which cannot be controlled in any other way. In the case of gooseberry mildew, the infested shoot tips should be cut off. Also remove all canes infested with raspberry cane disease and blackberry gall mite (see left).

Warning: Never throw any parts of diseased plants on to a compost heap! The best plan is to burn them.

Water jets and plant brews: If harmful pests appear in great numbers, you could try to wash them off the plants with a strong jet of water. If this does not work, spray the plants with herb brews (see p. 36).

Warning: Some herbal brews are toxic to bees (for example, quassia brew, mare's tail brew). Never use these brews when the plant is flowering!

Biological preparations on sale: Fortunately, biological agents for fortifying plants and preventing infestation with pests are now available in the gardening trade. In keeping with new plant protection laws, they have to be tested before release on the market, just like the traditional chemical agents. You can use them without any qualms but always follow the manufacturer's instructions and always keep them out of the reach of children and pets. Before using them, make sure that the agents contained in them are not harmful to useful insects and are non-toxic to fish or bees.

Pests and diseases of gooseberries, grapevines and red/white/blackcurrants	
	***American gooseberry mildew:*** The leaves and shoots are covered in a whitish film which later turns brown. The fruit is inedible and spotty. Prevention: Grow resistant varieties; shorten all shoot tips by 10 cm (4 in) during the autumn. Control: Cut off all infested parts and destroy them immediately.
	***Mildew (grapevines):*** A flour-like white film on both sides of leaves, also on young fruit. Prevention: Prune in autumn; do not place in damp positions. Spray prophylactically during the autumn and from the first month of spring onwards. Control: Not possible.
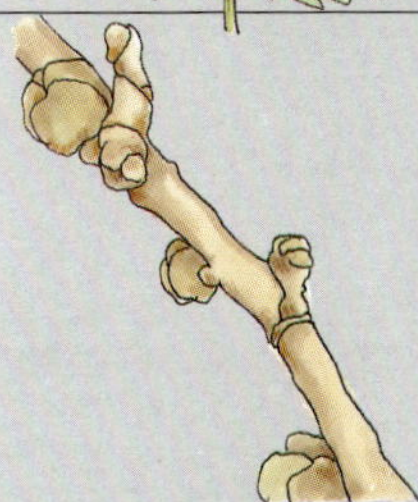	***Blackcurrant gall mite:*** As early as winter, you will see signs of unnaturally swollen roundish buds in blackcurrants. The buds do not unfold but dry up. Control: Immediately break off all swollen buds and cut off all shoots that bear such buds just above the ground.
	***Aphids (red/white/blackcurrants):*** Reddish blisters on the uppersides of leaves, soon spreading to the entire leaf. Minute insects on the undersides of leaves, practically invisible to the naked eye. Prevention: Not necessary as damage is not extensive. Cut off and burn infested leaves in the spring.
	***Coral spot (redcurrants):*** A reddish-brown film on the undersides of the leaves and falling leaves. Prevention: Thin out bushes after harvesting the fruit. Avoid the vicinity of pines where the rust overwinters. After flowering and fruit picking, spray with agents to prevent fungal infestation. Underplant wormwood. Control: Not possible.

Prevention

Encourage useful insects
Useful insects, the most important helpers in the battle against pests, require suitable hiding and overwintering quarters in your garden. There are several ways to encourage them.

A lacewing box
(illustration 1)
Lacewings overwinter as adult insects. You can take avantage of this fact by bringing these insects into your garden in a special catching box.
Build a box with sides 30 cm (12 in) long, with the front and bottom containing louvered sections and one wall being removable.
Paint the box bright red or reddish-brown and fix it to a 1.8 m (72 in) high post.
During the first month of autumn, pack the box with wheat straw or hay. Stand the box at the edge of your village or town near a field or meadow. The louvered wall should be directed away from the prevailing wind. After the first frosts, remove the box and post and place them in your garden near your soft fruit bushes. In the spring, up to 1,000 lacewing larvae will emerge to devour aphids and caterpillars.

Hiding places for earwigs
(illustration 2)
Earwigs tend to hide in a dark place during the daytime. During the night, they go out hunting for aphids. If you are able to offer them a comfortable place to hide near their source of food, they can easily be employed as helpers in the battle against aphids.
Pull a piece of wire through the drainage hole of a flowerpot.

1 A lacewing box serves as winter quarters for these insects.

Secure the wire on the inside with a small piece of wood. Stuff the inside of the pot with hay or wood shavings and hang it like a bell among your soft fruit bushes.

Winter quarters for useful insects
Ichneumon flies and other useful insects require sheltered,

2 Flowerpots make good hiding places for earwigs.

3 Logs with holes make good winter quarters for ichneumon flies.

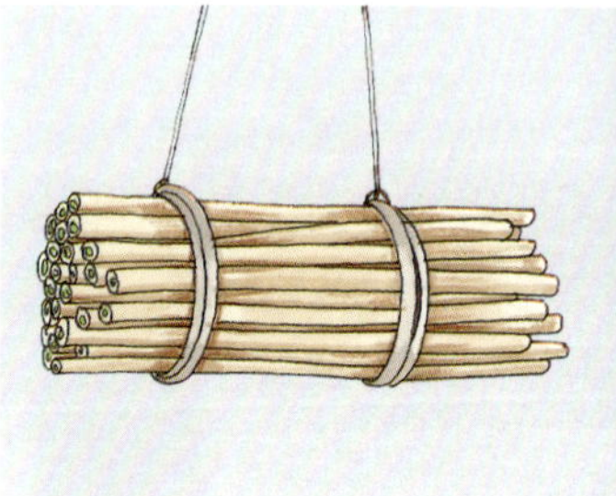

4 Bundles of reeds provide safe overwintering shelter for many useful insects.

protected winter quarters which they are unable to find in areas such as new housing estates and anywhere where there are no old barns or sheds or old trees.
Method 1 – Log of wood
(illustration 3)
Use a 3-mm gauge wood drill to make several holes set close together in each end of the log, drilling as deep as possible. Hang the log in a sheltered position.
Method 2 – Bundle of reeds
(illustration 4)
Cut reeds or pieces of bamboo into 20 cm (8 in) long sections and tie them tightly together. Hang the bundle in a sheltered, dry place.

Mechanical defences against pests and diseases

Relatively simple, traditional mechanical methods make it possible to prevent infestation by pests or diseases.

Sticky ring

(illustration 5)

Ants favour standards as places to establish colonies of aphids from which to obtain honeydew. To prevent this, fix sticky rings (available in the gardening trade) around the stems and support stakes of standards. These will also successfully ward off caterpillars. Make sure that the string used for tying these on is not too tight, while at the same time not loose enough for the ants to squeeze underneath.

Slug and snail fence

(illustration 6)

Slugs and snails just love strawberry beds. The safest protection is a slug and snail fence. This can be bought ready-made or you can make your own. You will require 20 cm (8 in) wide strips of zinc. Make a curve along the upper edge of the metal, forming a strip about 4 cm (1½ in) wide and bent at an angle of 45 degrees, or solder on a strip at the same angle.

Remove all slugs and snails from the bed.

Now install the strips of zinc all around the bed and fix them firmly in the soil. Make sure the joins are all tightly closed. Weeds and grass should never be allowed to hang over this fence or they will provide a "ladder" for slugs and snails to climb over. Another alternative is a solar-energy-powered electric slug fence which can be set up at a distance of 10 cm (4 in) on insulators fixed to planks all around the bed.

5 Sticky rings prevent ants from creating aphid colonies.

6 A fence made of zinc strips keeps slugs and snails away.

7 A strawberry collar prevents infestation by fungal infection.

A strawberry collar

(illustration 7)

Strawberries are very susceptible to attack by grey mould and other fungal infections if their leaves are in contact with damp soil. This can be prevented through the installation of a strawberry collar. From strong cardboard, cut a disc with a diameter corresponding to the width of the plant. Cut a slit from the edge to the centre and cut out a hole in the centre. Push the collar underneath the plant.

NB: You can buy ready-made strawberry collars.

Nets

To prevent the entire fruit harvest being gobbled up by greedy birds before you can pick it, it is a good idea to spread nets across the bushes. Red/white/blackcurrants, grapevines and blueberries are particularly at risk. Spread the nets over a frame made of posts and battens to prevent damaging the new shoots when removing the nets later on. The frame can be removed in early winter.

Warning: Use only very fine-mesh netting (30 x 30 mm). Birds often become caught in wide-mesh netting and die a lingering death. Pull the nets fairly taut.

Scarecrows

These homemade, usually fairly human-looking figures are probably the best-known form of mechanical plant protection. It need not be a figure, of course, the main thing is that it flaps about and makes a noise. Strips of silver foil or empty yoghurt containers hung up in the bushes will do just as well.

Healthy plants, delicious fruit

Soft fruit plants can be decorative additions to the garden. Their delicate flowers and brilliantly coloured fruit will make any vegetable garden or border look attractive. In reality, very little effort is required to make them grow well and produce a rich crop of fruit every year.

Glossary of keywords

The following pages give detailed instructions on care with emphasis on:

Name: The common name is given first, followed by the botanical one. Alternative names, if any, are also given.

Shape of growth: The outer appearance of the plant is always given.

Flower: What the flowers look like and when they appear.

Fruit: Details on the appearance of the fruit and when it should be ripe as well as when you can pick it.

Flavour: Are the berries sweet or sharp? This will also tell you about variations in the flavours of different varieties.

Contents: Tells you about the most important vitamins, minerals, etc. contained in the fruit.

Cuisine: Practical tips on processing soft fruit; whether it is suitable for freezing.

Suitable for: Advice on the way to plant and grow soft fruit in the garden or on patios or balconies. You will find out, for example, whether a particular species of soft fruit is suitable for a large container or for espaliers and pergolas.

Position: The most suitable position for your soft fruit.

Soil: The ideal soil and how you can improve it. (Pages 8 and 9 will tell you anything else you need to know about soil.)

Climate: Is the species of soft fruit suitable for elevated regions? In what area will it thrive best?

Pollination: Whether the plant needs another plant for pollination purposes.

Planting: Important tips on correct planting, for example the correct time and spacing.

Fertilizing: Advice on what to use and when.

Care: How to care for particular species throughout the year.

Cutting back: The correct way to prune and when.

Propagation: Information on the best method of propagation to use for particular types of soft fruit.

Plant protection: Information on the diseases to which individual soft fruit species are most susceptible, including tips on prevention and treatment (see also pp. 34-7).

Varieties: I have only given the names of recommended varieties, together with a description of their special characteristics, as there are very many different varieties, some of them regional.

My tip: Advice and tips from the author's own personal experience.

Soft fruit species at a glance

Strawberries in an urn
Strawberries will flourish just as well in an urn as in a bed. Planted in an attractive container, they form a decorative, eyecatching feature when grouped together with rosemary (left) and lavender (right).

Strawberries ripen from the last month of spring to the second month of autumn.

Strawberry flowers appear from the second month of spring onwards.

Strawberry

Fragaria x *ananassa*

Shape of growth: Low-growing, leafy plant, with leaves growing from a heart. Most varieties form runners which produce several small young plants. Alpine strawberries (*F. vesca* var. *semperflorens*) do not form any runners and flower and bear fruit from the last month of spring to the middle of autumn. Climbing and hanging strawberries form runners up to 1.5 m (60 in) long. Strawberries are easy to cultivate in pots and will bear fruit for two years. More recently, woodland strawberries from France have appeared on sale.
Flower: The buds begin to form in the first month of autumn; the white flowers appear in the second month of spring.
Fruit: Red fruits ripen from the end of spring to the middle of autumn. They comprise a thickened flower receptacle. The surface of the fruit is covered in tiny seeds called achenes.
Flavour: The older varieties and alpine strawberries are tastiest.
Contents: Lots of vitamin C (65 mg/100g), fructose, potassium.
Cuisine: For eating raw or making into jams, flans, jellies, juice. Varieties with firm flesh are suitable for freezing.
Suitable for: Growing in beds, large containers, strawberry barrel; alpines as an edging to a border; climbing and hanging strawberries on patios or balconies; varieties which produce lots of runners make good ground-cover.
Position: Sunny – vital for the fruit to develop its full flavour and the plants to be resistant to disease.
Soil: No particular requirements. The best soil is deep, humus-rich soil with a pH factor of 5-7.
Climate: Will flourish in almost any climate. Protection will be needed in regions with late frosts in the spring – use slit plastic sheets or matting.
Pollination: Self-pollinating except for a very few varieties. The yield is better if two different varieties are planted together.
Planting: Large fruit varieties during the second month of summer, at the latest by the middle of the last month of summer. Spaced about 30 cm (12 in) apart. Alpine strawberries during the second and third months of spring, spaced 25-30 cm (10-12 in) apart. Climbing and hanging strawberries should be planted in the spring. Renew plants every three to four years in an organically cultivated

garden. The fruit will decrease a little in size each year but the plants will produce the same quantity of fruit. Planting in a mixed culture has proved favourable.
Important: Buy only healthy, virus-free plants.
Fertilizing: Work in plenty of compost or organic fertilizer when planting. Add a little grit in very light soils. After the harvest, spread compost or organic fertilizer between the rows. Never fertilize when in flower.
Care: Water regularly after planting, including from the time of flowering until harvest. Loosen the surface of the soil a little between the plants, making sure the roots are not damaged. Remove weeds. Mulch with straw or other suitable material or use mulching sheets. Place a thick layer of straw under the berries before they start ripening. This will prevent them from getting dirty and make them more inaccessible to slugs, snails and woodlice.
Cutting: Cut back the leaves after the harvest (see p. 24). Mow alpine and wild strawberries.
Propagation: From strong, healthy young plants on the runners of parent plants which produced large amounts of fruit (see p. 32). Make sure you use healthy parent plants as the runners are able to pass on many diseases. Propagating climbing strawberries is very difficult.
Plant protection: Particularly susceptible to attack by fungal infection and also by pests and diseases of the roots. With the right care and a sunny, well-ventilated position, this risk can be greatly reduced. Spray with biological agents as a preventive from spring through to flowering time (see p. 36). The best prevention is always to grow resistant varieties.
Varieties: New cultivars are introduced almost every year but it is probably better to keep to the tastier, well tried and tested varieties.
Strawberries with large fruit: *Early*: "Zefyr", "Regina", "Elvira"; *Medium early*: "Marieva", "Vigerla", "Tenira", "Cambridge Regent", "Cambridge Early Pine", "Cambridge Favourite", "Senga Gigana"; *Late*: "Elisata", "Red Gauntlet", "Senga Sengana".
Varieties producing several crops: "Macherauchs Dauerernte", "Revada", "Hummi Genata", "Ostara".
Alpines: "Rimona Hummi" (quite large), "Rugen", "Baron Solemacher" (small).

My tip: Regularly cut off the runners of plants that you are not going to use for propagation purposes. Vigorous production of runners tends to weaken the parent plant and the harvest is reduced.

Climbing strawberries should be planted in the spring.

Blueberries flower in the third month of spring.

Blueberries require acid soil.

Cultivated blueberry
Vaccinium corymbosum

Shape of growth: Spreading bushes up to 1.5 m (60 in) tall. In some varieties, red foliage in the autumn.
Flower: Red-white, bell-shaped flowers in the last month of spring.
Fruit: Large blue berries ripen from the middle of the first month of summer until the end of the first month of autumn. The juice does not stain, unlike that of forest blueberries.
Flavour: Strong and very tasty, sweeter than that of wild blueberries.
Contents: Vitamin C (about 25 mg/100 g), vitamins A and B.
Cuisine: Eaten fresh and raw, also made into flans, preserves, jam and juice. Excellent for freezing.
Suitable for: Medium-high hedge; ornamental bush. The variety "Top Hat" is ideal for growing in pots.
Position: Full sunlight.
Soil: Will require acidic, woodland-type soil (pH factor 4-5).
Climate: Fairly undemanding; copes with temperatures as low as minus 25° C (minus 13° F).
Pollination: Self-pollinating but will yield more fruit if two different varieties are grown side by side.
Planting: During the autumn or second month of spring. The planting hole should be 1 x 1 m (40 x 40 in) wide, 50 cm (20 x 20 in) deep. Fill with ericaceous compost or peat and forest soil, then plant. Set the plant about 5 cm (2 in) deeper than it was in the nursery. In areas with lime-rich soil, line the hole with a perforated sheet of polythene. Spacing: 1.4-2 m (56-80 in).
Fertilizing: Feed only in autumn with well-rotted compost lightly worked in. Check the pH factor of the soil.
Care: A thick layer of mulch made of grass cuttings, dead leaves, straw or conifer needles. Use only rainwater for watering. Protect from hungry birds with fine-mesh netting.
Cutting: Not until after the fifth year. Then cut the oldest shoots near the ground or above a young shoot.
Propagation: By layering.
Plant protection: Pests and diseases rarely occur.
Varieties: *Early*: "Bluetta"; *Medium early*: "Bluecrop"; *Late*: "Berkeley", "Herbert", "Jersey", "Coville"; *Very abundant crop*: "Dixi".

My tip: Bird netting is very difficult to remove. It is better to create a homemade cage out of battens and fine-mesh wire.

Cranberries make a delicious accompaniment to game and other meat.

Cultivated cranberries
Vaccinium vitis-idaea

Shape of growth: Low-growing, about 15 cm (6 in) tall, evergreen bush which forms 1 m (40 in) long shoots and grows as groundcover. The leaves turn red in the autumn.
Flower: Pink flowers from the third month of spring to the middle of summer.
Fruit: Spherical red berries in two crops – smaller amounts in mid-summer; large amounts in mid to late autumn.
Flavour: sharp, woody.
Contents: Lots of vitamin C, some vitamin B, citric acid, potassium.
Cuisine: Not suitable for consuming raw. As a preserve with game and other meats. For juice and jam (mixed with other, sweeter fruits if desired).
Suitable for: In a bed in a vegetable garden, as groundcover in an ornamental garden, particularly under azaleas and rhododendrons.
Position: In full sunlight or semi-shade.
Soil: As poor and low in nutrients as possible. Also sandy or stony soils that dry out easily. pH factor 4.5-5.5.
Climate: Prefers areas with rougher weather.
Pollination: Self-pollinating. Pollinated also by honeybees and bumble bees.
Planting: During autumn or the last month of winter/first month of spring. Place the plant a little deeper in the soil than it was in the nursery. Work in a little acid peat. Spacing: 20-25 cm (8-10 in).
Fertilizing: Very sparingly. *Note:* Very sensitive to an accumulation of salts! Just a little compost in the autumn is best.
Care: Hardly any. Only water during long periods of drought. Mulch with peat, wood shavings and conifer needles.
Cutting: Not necessary. Only cut off the shoots protruding from the bed.
Propagation: Forms small plants on runners, which can be planted in another bed during the spring.
Plant protection: *Phytophthora* decay may occur if fertilized too much!
Varieties: "Blue Crop", "Bluetta", "Herbert", "Spartan".

My tip: A large-fruited cranberry is now available. The berries are larger than the usual cultivated cranberries and grow on single stems. The flavour, content and use are the same, as is care. The only difference is that this large variety likes an even drier environment.

Currant bushes flower from the first month of spring onwards.

Late variety: "Heinemanns Rote Spätlese".

Currants
(red/black/white)
Ribes spp.

Shape of growth: Bushes can attain a height and width of 2 m (80 in). The white and red varieties produce new shoots from the rootstock; the black varieties produce new shoots from the lower parts of older branches.
Flower: Small green flowers in racemes from the beginning of spring.
Fruit: Dense, up to 15 cm (6 in) long racemes, on two- to three-year-old wood in white and red varieties, and on one-year-old wood in blackcurrants. Early varieties ripen in early summer; late ones in late summer.
Flavour: Redcurrants sharp to sweet; whitecurrants a little less acidic. Blackcurrants are less sweet, have a strong, woody flavour and are not often eaten raw.
Contents: Vitamin C (red, white 40 mg/100 g; black 170 mg/100 g), citric acid, malic acid, tartaric acid, pectin.
Cuisine: red- and whitecurrants are ideal fresh and for jams, juice, liqueur. Blackcurrants for jams, juice and wine. All varieties are suitable for freezing.
Suitable for: Planting in rows. Espaliers are only worthwhile if you are growing large numbers of bushes. As standards, in large containers (at least 50 litres), also on patios and balconies.
Position: Sunny or the fruit will remain sour.
Soil: Medium heavy, nutrient-rich, slightly acid soils (pH 5.5-6). Sandy soils are less suitable as the bushes require regular watering.
Climate: Most climates. Late varieties are recommended for higher altitudes because of the risk of frost in spring.
Pollination: Red and white varieties are self-pollinating, but better harvests are obtained if several different varieties are grown side by side. Both self-pollinating and non-self-pollinating varieties can be found among blackcurrants. The best practice is always to plant at least two different varieties. In cool, wet weather during flowering time you can aid pollination by shaking the bushes several times a day.
Planting: Best in autumn. During spring only until the end of the first month. Red and white varieties should be planted 2 cm (¾ in) deeper than in the nursery; black varieties about 10 cm (4 in) deeper. Spacing: 1.5 m (60 in) for red and white; 2 m (80 in) for black varieties.

A milder flavour than the red varieties: "Weisse Versailler".

Blackcurrants have a woody flavour.

Fertilizing: During the autumn, superficially rake in a 5 cm (2 in) thick layer of half-rotted compost (be careful of the shallow roots). During the spring, the same amount of rotted compost, cow dung or horse or chicken manure can be worked in. If you have neither compost nor manure to hand, fertilize with fermented nettle brew every two weeks from the second month of spring, and fertilize with a liquid horn-blood-bonemeal preparation in the first month of spring.
Care: Mulch all year round as moist soil is very important.
Cutting: For red and white varieties, after the harvest cut off three-year-old shoots (dark wood) close to the ground. For blackcurrants, cut off the shoots that have borne fruit. Cut off all the inward-growing branches in all varieties to ensure that the plants will receive enough light. Cutting is also possible in late autumn, but the harvest will then be smaller the following year compared to the harvest after a summer cut.
Standards: The crown should never have more than eight well-distributed branches which should be cut back to six buds each after the harvest. Cut back laterals to four buds.
Propagation: Red- and whitecurrants from cuttings; blackcurrants by layering downward-hanging laterals.
Plant protection: Do not plant too close together. From the first month of spring to three weeks before the harvest, spray every four weeks with mare's tail brew as a preventive against fungal infection. Break off any extremely fat buds during early spring as they may contain blackcurrant gall mites. Use fine-mesh netting to protect plant buds from hungry birds, or, better still, hang fluttering objects in the branches to discourage them.
Varieties: *Red*: "Red Lake", "Heros" (*early*), "Laxton's No 1", "Jonkheer van Tets", "Red Lake" (*medium*), "Heinemanns Rote Spätlese" (*late*).
White: "Weisse aus Jüterborg" (*early*), "White Versailles" (*medium*).
Black: "Laxton's Giant", "Strata" (*early*), "Wellington" (*medium*), "Amos Black", "Baldwin" (*late*).

My tip: Bind up bushes in snowy regions. Cut the string after flowering. This will protect the flowers and pollination will be more successful.

Raspberries can be picked from the second month of summer onwards.

Yellow raspberries: "Hauensteins Gelbe"

Raspberry
Rubus idaeus

Shape of growth: Canes up to 3 m (120 in) long, which die off in the autumn. Young shoots grow up during the first month of summer. These will bear next year's fruit.
Flower: Single, individually set flowers during the second and third months of spring.
Fruit: Slightly elongated, red (in some varieties yellow) "berries" that actually comprise many tiny fruits sitting on a cone. Harvest from the middle of summer onwards. Autumn raspberries can be picked until the first frosts.
Flavour: Pleasant, almost more sharp than sweet.
Contents: High in minerals, particularly potassium, phosphorus and iron. High amounts of citric acid and malic acid.
Cuisine: For eating fresh, for flans, jams, jellies, juice, liqueur and wine. Suitable for freezing.
Suitable for: Planting in rows along a fence or, better still, on an espalier (see p. 10).
Position: Sunny but also in semi-shade.
Soil: Relatively undemanding. Will also flourish in sandy, stony soil if it has been enriched with humus. The pH value should be 4.5-5.5. Raspberries do not like waterlogging!
Climate: Any climate. As they flower late, there is no risk from frost even in a harsh climate.
Pollination: Self-pollinating. Regular harvests and larger fruit can be obtained if several different varieties are planted side by side.
Planting: During autumn or early spring; container plants all year round. Plant immediately after purchase or keep moist as the roots will dry out very quickly. The shoot buds on roots should be kept 5 cm (2 in) under the soil. After planting, shorten the canes to 50 cm (20 in). Space between plants: 20 cm (8 in).
Fertilizing: During the autumn mulch with a thick layer of half-rotted manure – pig manure is best. If you have no access to animal manure, use horn-blood-bonemeal sprinkled on the soil in early spring and then covered with mulch. Magnesium is very important so sprinkle one shovelful of woodash per square metre every year.
Care: Mulch with dead leaves, conifer needles, straw or half-rotted compost. Do not use bark mulch as it will suppress the growth of new shoots. Underplant with peas, beans, clover or marigolds (*Calendula*).

Cutting: Cut off canes that have borne fruit close to the ground in the autumn. Thin out young canes to about ten plants per metre. Do not cut off the harvested canes of varieties that bear fruit twice or those of autumn raspberries (e.g. "Autumn Bliss") until winter. Canes that are too long can be cut back to 1.5 m (60 in) during the last month of spring. They will branch out and bear fruit a little later. Take out weaker canes during the first month of spring.

Propagation: From suckers produced by the roots.

Plant protection: The most feared problem is raspberry cane disease. Sick canes should be cut off immediately and burned. As a preventive, spray with mare's tail brew from the first month of spring onwards.

Varieties: *Early*: "Malling Promise"; *Medium early*: "Glen Clova", "Malling Jewel", "Meeker", "Schönemann", "Zefa 1", "Zefa 2"; *Late* (twice fruiting): "Zefa 3", "Heritage", "Norfolk Giant". *Autumn raspberry:* (bears fruit from the second month of summer until the middle of autumn on one-year-old wood): "Autumn Bliss"; *Yellow fruit:* "Goldtraube".

Crosses: The tayberry is a cross between the raspberry and blackberry. The fruit looks like an over-sized raspberry and has a stronger, sharper flavour.

"Malling Promise" is very sweet and ripens early.

Gooseberries contain lots of vitamin C.

Gooseberries

Ribes uva-crispa var. *sativum*

Shape of growth: Woody bushes, up to 1.5 m (60 in) tall and 1.5 m (60 in) wide. The shoots have sharp thorns so be careful when harvesting.
Flower: Grows singly or in racemes. Flowers are small and inconspicuous but quite pretty (see p. 51). They appear from the beginning of the second month of spring.
Fruit: The berries are ripe from the middle of the first month of summer. They are round, yellowish-green, green or red with varying numbers of bristles.
Flavour: mildly sharp, also sweet when fully ripe, depending on the variety. "White" varieties (more yellow than green) have most flavour.
Contents: Lots of vitamin C (about 35 mg/100 g), fructose and citric acid.
Cuisine: Unripe and half-ripe fruit for flans and preserves; ripe fruit for eating fresh, for jams and gooseberry wine. Also suitable for freezing.
Suitable for: Planting in rows or as individual bushes in vegetable or ornamental gardens, also together with currant bushes; two gooseberry bushes will be quite adequate for a family of four. Standards are very attractive and will bear lots of fruit. They will also grow in large containers (50 litres/11 gal), but are sensitive to wind when heavy with fruit (support with at least two strong stakes).
Position: Best in a sunny position with a little shade at noon to prevent sunburn.
Soil: Prefers loamy, nutrient-rich soil with some lime. Sandy soils should be improved with plenty of humus.
Climate: Undemanding. At higher altitudes there is a risk to sensitive flowers from late frosts. Here it is better to plant a late variety.
Pollination: Self-pollinating. Often the male pollen is ripe before the female stigma is fully developed, so it is a good idea to plant bushes of two different varieties, which tend to flower about two weeks apart, side by side.
Planting: Best in autumn or in very early spring. Place the plant at the same depth as it was in the tree nursery. Cut back the shoots to about 30 cm (12 in). Spacing of bushes: 1.5-2 m (60-80 in); for standards at least 1.5 m (60 in) or, better still, 1.8 m (72 in).
Fertilizing: During the autumn, place a 15 cm (6 in) thick layer of compost or well-rotted

Gooseberry flowers are small but very pretty.

Yellow gooseberries are very popular.

manure under the bushes, only superficially raked in (gooseberries have shallow roots). Add extra fertilizer by using fermented nettle or borage brew in the spring after flowering and in summer after the harvest, or fertilize with a horn-blood-bonemeal preparation.

Care: Mulch all year round to avoid loss of moisture.

Cutting: To make harvesting easier, the bush should not have more than ten to twelve one- to two-year-old shoots, which means cutting back every year. Older shoots (darker wood) should be cut back immediately after the harvest, as should any superfluous young shoots. Shorten all the shoots of varieties susceptible to mildew by about 10 cm (4 in). Allow eight long shoots of standards to remain and thin out lateral shoots to make harvesting easier.

Propagation: By layering downward-hanging laterals.

Plant protection: Spray soft soap solution to combat aphids or use plant brews (see p. 36). Shorten the tips of all shoots by about 10 cm (4 in) in the autumn as a prevention against the dreaded gooseberry mildew, even if the plant shows no signs of infestation. The shoot tips are where the fungus spores like to overwinter. If the plant is infested with mildew (see p. 37), pick off and gather up all the infected fruit and destroy it. The fruit will be spotty and inedible! Cut off all infested parts and burn them. As a future prevention, plant mildew-resistant varieties.

Varieties: Early: "Bedford Red", "Broom Girl" (yellowish), "Invicta" (yellowish-green, mildew-resistant); Medium early: "Bedford Yellow", "Dornenlos" (reddish with only a few, soft thorns), "Careless", "Gunner"; *Late*: "Achilles" (dark red). More and more new, mildew-resistant varieties are being offered for sale in nurseries.

My tip: If you wish your gooseberry bushes to produce a particularly good harvest, you should remove half of the berries when they are half-ripe (use them for making jam or for freezing). The remaining fruit will be particularly large and sweet.

Jostaberries ripen gradually.

Jostaberry flowers are very pretty.

Jostaberry
Ribes x culverwellii

Shape of growth: The jostaberry is a cross between a blackcurrant and a gooseberry. The bush looks similar to the blackcurrant in shape and grows to about 2 m (80 in) tall and 2.5 m (100 in) wide. The shoots do not have thorns.
Flower: Small flowers appear from the first month of spring.
Fruit: The berries are slightly larger than blackcurrant berries but almost as dark and have no hairs. Generally, two to five berries hang on short racemes. Not all the berries are ripe at the same time so you can pick fruit several times from the first month of summer onwards.
Flavour: The rather strong taste of blackcurrants is rendered a little milder through the influence of the gooseberry.
Contents: Vitamin C (100 mg/100 g), citric acid and malic acid.
Cuisine: For eating raw, for jams, jellies and juice. Well suited to freezing.
Suitable for: Single bushes or as a hedge in a vegetable or ornamental garden. Goes well with currant and gooseberry bushes. Standards (rare) can also be grown in a large container.
Position: Requires plenty of sunlight.
Soil: Undemanding.
Climate: All climates.
Pollination: Self-pollinating.
Planting; During the autumn in well-loosened soil prepared with compost or well-rotted manure. Space the plants about 3 m (120 in) apart. The bushes will grow quickly and if placed too close together will obstruct one another which results in the berries not receiving enough sunlight.
Fertilizing: Spread a layer of compost underneath the bushes in autumn.
Care: Mulch all year round.
Cutting: Cutting back is not necessary. Thin out after the harvest or during the winter in later years. This is done to ensure that all berries receive enough sunlight.
Propagation: By layering hanging laterals.
Plant protection: Mainly resistant to blackcurrant gall mite and mildew. Falling leaf disease is unknown in this cross. If necessary, spray with a soft soap solution to combat aphids.
Varieties: None as this is a cross.

My tip: Do not harvest the berries until they are really quite dark and fully ripe. This is the only way to retain their full flavour.

Thornless blackberries are eminently suitable for espaliers.

Ripe blackberries are a deep blue in colour.

Blackberry

Rubus fruticosus

Shape of growth: Shoots 8 m (26 ft) long, with thorns. There is an upright variety which is cultivated like a raspberry.
Flower: White flowers from the end of spring to the end of summer.
Fruit: Roundish or slightly elongated "berries", red, then turning dark blue.
Flavour: Pleasantly sweet. Thornless varieties may have less flavour.
Contents: Vitamins A, B and C, iron and more magnesium than other berried fruits. Not a great deal of sugar.
Cuisine: For eating raw or as jams, juice, preserves. Good for freezing.
Suitable for: Espaliers along a sheltered south-facing wall or house wall, or free-standing espaliers in a very warm position. Thornless varieties can be grown on a pergola.
Position: A warm, sheltered position for maximum ripening of the fruit.
Soil: Undemanding. There is danger of frost damage only on very heavy, wet soils.
Climate: Do not plant in regions above 600 m (1,960 ft) as the shoots will freeze and die at minus 15° C (5° F).
Pollination: All varieties are self-pollinating.
Planting: When planting, cover the sensitive buds near the ground with up to 5 cm (2 in) of soil to protect them from frost damage. Spacing for varieties with thorns 4 m (160 in); 2 m (80 in) for thornless varieties; 50 cm (20 in) for upright ones.
Fertilizing: Use liquid horn-blood-bonemeal fertilizer during flowering. During autumn, cover the rootstocks with compost or rotted manure.
Care: Mulch during the summer; protect the roots from frost with a straw layer during the winter.
Cutting: Cut back the reserve shoots in the leaf axils, leaving four buds on each. These will produce the laterals that will later bear fruit. After the harvest, cut back both the canes that have borne fruit and new shoots, leaving four to eight vigorous young shoots. Regularly remove any extra shoots.
Propagation: By layering hanging laterals.
Plant protection: During the autumn, cut off and burn any canes with blackberry gall mite.
Varieties: "Theodor Reimers", "Black Satin", "Thornless Evergreen" (thornless), "Wilsons Early" (upright).

My tip: Regularly remove all shoots growing from the neck of the root or they will run riot.

"Blauer Burgunder" grapes and leaves showing their autumn colouring.

A lovely bunch of white grapes.

Grapevine
Vitis vinifera

Shape of growth: The grapevine is a climbing plant with fibrous, tough wood and light green, lobed leaves which turn beautiful colours in the autumn, depending on the variety.
Flower: Small green flowers on panicles during the last month of spring/first month of summer.
Fruit: Berries form in dense, large bunches and ripen during the first and second months of autumn. There are black (really blue) and white (really greenish-yellow) varieties, with or without seeds.
Flavour: Varies from one variety to another, from very sweet to sharp.
Content: Sugar, lots of potassium.
Cuisine: For eating raw, for making juice and wine. Dried as raisins.
Suitable for: An espalier on a house wall in a warm, sheltered position; for climbing over a pergola, fence or wall. A grapevine will grow in a large container on a balcony but will not live as long as one planted in the ground.
Position: Very sunny; protect from too much moisture.
Soil: Loose, warm soil containing humus and lime is optimal. Avoid any waterlogging!
Climate: Requires warmth. In a really sheltered position it will flourish at altitudes of up to 800 m (2,620 ft). A dry climate is preferable to a rainy one. Too much moisture brings a risk of mildew.
Pollination: Self-pollinating.
Planting: During the spring and right into the summer, plant as large container plants. As ground plants, place plenty of compost in a 40 cm (16 in) deep planting hole and mix in some lime. Builders' rubble right at the bottom is ideal as it makes the soil permeable and contains lime. If several vines are grown on one wall, space them 3-5 m (120-200 in) apart. For further details on planting, see page 17.
Fertilizing: Place a thick layer of compost or well-rotted manure around the roots in the autumn. Add lime annually to soils that contain little chalk.
Care: Always mulch so that the soil does not dry out. If the plant is growing near to a building, do not forget to water it well as it will probably receive too little water even when it is raining. Water the roots only as wet leaves and fruit will invite fungal infections.
Cutting: Cut the vine back to about 50 cm (20 in)

during the first year after planting. Keep only three to four of the shoots that appear, which can later be tied to the espalier. Grapes will grow only on young shoots on two-year old wood. The fruit-bearing shoots should be cut back in the first month of spring (see p. 25). Pruning should be carried out during the winter. Grapevines will ooze sap if they are damaged during the growing phase of their cycle and this weakens the plant.

Propagation: Possible from cuttings but rather difficult. Vines should be grafted as this is the only way to obtain large healthy plants.

Plant protection: Susceptible to fungal infections, particularly during wet summers. A position sheltered from rain, under overhanging eaves for example, would be ideal. Spray with biological fungicidal agents during the autumn after leaf fall and again from spring into late summer, every four weeks. When the grapes are ripe, protect them from birds.

Varieties: *Black*: "Black Alicante", "Black Hamburgh", "Blue Portuguese", "Black Prince"; *White:* "Aubergine Oberlin", "Chasselas D'Or", "Golden Queen", Perle de Czaba", "Früher Malinger", "Muskat Gutedel".

A very sunny position is essential for an abundant harvest.

The kiwi fruit is a climbing plant with long shoots.

Kiwi fruit or Chinese gooseberry

Actinidia chinensis

Shape of growth: A creeper with shoots up to 10 m (400 in) long. Large, deep green, hairy leaves and brown, hairy shoots.
Flower: During the last month of spring/first month of autumn. Female flowers are pure white to a delicate cream, with a diameter of up to 5 cm (2 in), a ray-shaped style and four to eight false umbels. The male flowers are smaller and cream-coloured, with several bunches of anthers.
Fruit: Ripe during the last month of autumn. A tough, brown, slightly hairy skin and juicy green flesh with lots of seeds. The fruit of the variety "Weiki" is smaller and its skin can be eaten.
Flavour: Sharp to sweet.
Contents: Vitamin C (about 60 mg/100 g), potassium and calcium.
Cuisine: For eating raw, but only after being stored for about a month. For cooking, for preserves, flans and ice cream. Do not freeze.
Suitable for: An espalier, preferably a sheltered south-west-facing wall. Can also be trained over a pergola.
Position: Warm, sunny, sheltered from wind.
Soil: Nutrient-rich. Preferably slightly acid, pH value 4.5-5.5. There is a risk of chlorosis in soil containing a lot of lime.

Kiwi fruit flowers are pure white to creamy white.

Kiwi fruits are full of vitamins.

Climate: Only in sheltered positions. Young shoots do not cope well with temperatures below minus 10° C (14° F). "Weiki" is completely hardy and resistant to frost, but the fruits will not have time to ripen properly at high altitudes.
Pollination: Pollinated by bees. Some varieties are self-pollinating. With other varieties, at least one male plant will have to be planted in a group of four female plants.
Planting: From mid-spring onwards to avoid the risk of frosts. Loosen the soil to two spades' depth before planting. If the pH value is above 6, the soil from the hole should be mixed with peat. For detailed instructions on espaliers, see page 10. Spacing: 3-4 m (120-160 in).
Fertilizing: From the fourth year onwards the plant will produce full crops of fruit and will require a thick layer of compost or rotted manure around the roots every year. In addition, give it a horn-blood-bonemeal mixture as a liquid fertilizer in the spring. After flowering, fertilize with fermented nettle or borage brew every two weeks.
Care: You will have to water plants growing close to a building. A layer of mulch will retain moisture. Dryness will cause the fruit to drop off.
Cutting: It is mainly the shoots which develop from the first six buds of the main and secondary shoots that will bear fruit. Encouraging this fruit-bearing wood requires the regular cutting off of all shoot extensions that grow above the sixth leaf (see p. 25). From the fifth year onwards, during the winter cut off all shoots that are older than three years as fruit will mainly grow on two-year-old wood.
Propagation: Kiwi fruit plants have to be grafted on to robust stocks in order to survive in the European climate.
Plant protection: It is generally unaffected by diseases and pests in a temperate zone. If the leaves turn yellow, give the plant an iron preparation and also check the pH factor of the soil.
Varieties: *Large-fruited chinensis varieties*: "Hayward", "Ashoka", "Zealand", "Monty", "Abbot" (all requiring cross-pollination), "Jenny" (self-pollinating); *Small-fruited, smooth-skinned Arguta variety*: "Weiki" (requiring cross-pollination) is at present the only variety on sale.

My tip: Kiwi fruits will be ripe within a few days after picking if they are stored in a plastic bag together with one apple.

Never eat raw elderberries!

Scented, creamy white elderflowers.

Elderberry
Sambucus nigra

Shape of growth: The elderberry bush may developinto a 6 m (20 ft) tall, widely spreading tree.
Flower: Creamy-white, scented flower umbels in early summer.
Fruit: Black fruit umbels on dark red stalks, which gradually ripen from the end of summer onwards.
Flavour: strong, woody.
Contents: Flower: lots of vitamin C, etheric oil, fruit acid; Berries: lots of vitamins A, B and C.
Cuisine: The flowers are used for the manufacture of cordial and elderberry "champagne". Do not eat the berries raw as they are slightly toxic. When they are cooked they are suitable for juice, jellies, jams and wine.
Suitable for: Natural hedges, as a garden tree, to camouflage an ugly shed, to provide shade for a compost heap.
Position: Will thrive in a sunny or shady position.
Soil: Undemanding, will grow anywhere.
Climate: Hardy, resistant to frost, no limitations.
Pollination: Self-pollinating.
Planting: Will often seed itself. Plant young plants in the autumn.
Fertilizing: Not necessary; give a little compost or manure only on sandy soils.
Care: Apart from some thinning out, no care is required.
Cutting: This is basically unnecessary. If you regularly thin out branches hanging down to the ground during the autumn, however, you will obtain larger berries. If an elderberry bush is very old it should be cut back to 30 cm (12 in) above the ground in the winter; or, if a tree, to 20 cm (8 in) from the trunk.
Propagation: From seed.
Plant protection: Hardly susceptible at all to pests or diseases. If the plant suffers from falling leaves, hose down several times with a vigorous jet of water.
Varieties: "Haschberg", "Donau". Wild plants that have colonized your garden by themselves are just as good.
Warning: Raw berries and uncooked juice should not be consumed as they may cause nausea and vomiting. The bark contains small quantities of prussic acid so it is also toxic.

My tip: Elderberry is used in herbal medicine. Tea made from the flowers encourages sweating in people with fevers and colds. The leaves and bark also have healing properties but should not be used by laypersons as the wrong doses can cause poisoning.

Filberts have closed husks.

Male flowers: the long, yellow lambs'tails.

Hazelnut
Corylus avellana

Shape of growth: Bushes up to 7 m (24 ft) tall and 4 m (160 in) wide.
Flower: Flowers appear on young wood from mid-winter onwards. Only the two red stigmata of the female flowers are visible; the male flowers are the long yellow "lambs' tails".
Fruit: This is not actually a berry at all (see note, p. 4). Pick nuts from the first month of autumn onwards. The kernels sit inside hard, light brown, oval or round shells enclosed in tough husks. There are two types: cobnuts with short, open husks and filberts with husks that are long and closed at the end. There are also a number of hybrids with short husks.
Flavour: nutty, mild.
Contents: Fat (60 g/ 100 g), carbohydrates, protein.
Cuisine: Snacks, biscuits, cake, liqueur.
Suitable for: Hedges or as individual bushes.
Position: Sunny to semi-shady, cool rather than warm (not south-facing).
Soil: Humus-rich.
Climate: The wood is completely hardy. However, the lambs' tails may freeze in severe frosts, so choose a sheltered position.
Pollination: Self-pollinating, so always plant a second bush of another variety.
Planting: During the autumn, dig a planting hole with a diameter of 50 cm (20 in) and 30 cm (12 in) deep. Cut back the roots before planting. Spacing in a hedge: 3-4 m (120-160 in).
Fertilizing: not required.
Care: Hardly any is necessary. Allow fallen leaves to lie under the bush.
Cutting: The nuts grow on young shoots so cut out the old shoots every winter. Bushes that are old and and have grown too big can be cut back to 50 cm (20 in) above the ground. In the spring, allow only the three strongest shoots on each main branch to remain.
Propagation: From cuttings or by layering hanging laterals.
Plant protection: Hardly any disease ever observed. The hazelnut borer, a beetle which tunnels into the nuts, tends to attack filberts. Early in the morning during the last month of spring/first month of summer, shake the branches over a large cloth to collect the beetles.
Varieties: *Cobnuts*: "Webb's Prize Cob", "Nottingham Prolific", "Halle Giant", "Cosford", "Daviana"; *Filberts*: "Kentish Cob", "Red Filbert".

Index

Numbers in **bold** indicate illustrations.

Index

Index

Author's note
This volume explains how to grow soft fruit organically. This includes instructions for the use of biological plant protection preparations. It is important to be careful when handling these substances: always follow the instructions and keep children and pets away when applying these substances. Wear gloves if you are using substances containing pyrethrum which must not be allowed to penetrate an open wound. Always store plant protection agents in such a way that they are inaccessible to children and pets.
This volume only discusses plants that have edible fruit. Nevertheless, we should like to point out that there is always a risk of confusing species and varieties of edible berries with the toxic ones of ornamental shrubs etc. (see p. 6). Particularly if you have young children, you should try to avoid growing ornamental shrubs which might be confused with edible soft fruit plants. Please also note that you should never eat raw elderberries as this may make you feel nauseous (see p. 58).
In recent times gardeners have been advised to take great care when handling animal products such as horn-blood-bonemeal. If you do use such products, do ensure that you obtain your supply from a reputable source and that it has been produced by a manufacturer who has complied with current legislation covering the production of such products. Always wear gloves when using such substances and always also make sure that children and pets do not touch them.

Photographic acknowledgements
De Cuveland: p. 51 left; Eisenbeiss: p. 53 right, 58 left, Laux: p. 8, 59 left; Lobl-Schreyer: p. 54 left; Mein Schöner Garten/Fischer: p. 43; Mein Schöner Garten/Gross: p. 57 right; Mein Schöner Garten/Stork: p. 56; Reinhard: p. 15, 35, 46 left; Sammer: p. 29; Scherz: p. 2 right; Silvestris/Sauer: p. 30 top; Strauss: all other photos.

This edition published 1995 by
Merehurst Limited
Ferry House, 51-57 Lacy Road,
Putney, London SW15 1PR

ISBN 1 85391 538 6

A catalogue record for this book is available from the British Library.

Translated by Astrid Mick
Edited by Lesley Young
Design and typesetting by Paul Cooper
Printed in Hong Kong by Wing King Tong